To the men and women of Boeing

"Let no new improvement in flying and flying equipment pass us by."

– William E. Boeing, founder
The Boeing Company, 1929. –

George Conrad Westervelt and William Edward "Bill" Boeing pose with the B&W Model 1 in front of Bill Boeing's Lake Union boathouse. *Boeing Historical Archives*

Donald Douglas Snr, the aviation industry's and one of the world's greatest industrialists, poses with the DC-4. This was his favorite photo. *McDonnell Douglas*

"Dream no small dream; it lacks magic. Dream large. Then make the dream real."

– Donald Douglas Snr –

Boeing 787 Dreamliner – Flying Redefined

By Guy Norris, Geoffrey Thomas, Mark Wagner and Christine Forbes Smith

First edition published in October 2005

Aerospace Technical Publications International Pty Ltd
P.O. Box 8205
Perth Business Centre
Stirling Street Post Office, Perth
Western Australia 6849
Tel: + 61 41 793 6610
Fax:+ 61 89 403 6113
Geoffreythomas@iinet.net.au
Christinefs@bigpond.com

Authors:	Guy Norris, Geoffrey Thomas, Mark Wagner and Christine Forbes Smith
Editor:	Christine Forbes Smith
Art Work/Graphs:	Juanita Franzi - Aero Art Publications
Photographers:	Mark Wagner, Geoffrey Thomas, Captain Kevin Tate, Joe Walker, Charlie Atterbury and John Dibbs (planepix.com) All chapter start photos by Mark Wagner and Geoffrey Thomas.
Photo Library:	Aviation Images Ltd (Mark Wagner) aviation-images.com 42-B,Queens Road, Wimbledon, London SW19 8LR,England G.B. Tel: +44 20-8944-5225 Fax: +44 20-8944-5335 pictures@aviation-images.com
Style Editor:	Kerry Coyle
Technical Editing:	Simon Wells
Design Concept:	Kym Weir-Smith - 303 Advertising, Perth
Layout, Typesetting and Scanning:	PK Print Pty Ltd 23 Emplacement Crescent, Hamilton Hill Western Australia 6163 Ph: +61 8 9336 3800 Fax: +61 8 9336 3811 jobs@pkprint.com.au www.pkprint.com

ISBN 0-9752341-2-9
Cover images: Boeing
Back cover images: Boeing

Contents

Northwest Airlines Inc ordered up to 68 787s on 5 May 2005. *Boeing*

Acknowledgments

It is impossible to put into words the gratitude we feel to those who have helped bring *Boeing 787 Dreamliner – Flying Redefined* to lift-off.

Assistance has ranged from encouragement from Alan Mulally (President and CEO of Boeing Commercial Airplanes (BCA)), Sir Rod Eddington (former Chief Executive Officer of British Airways, Ansett Airlines and Cathay Pacific Airways), John Poynton (founder of Azure Capital Pty Ltd), Ralph Norris (former Managing Director and CEO of Air New Zealand) and Tom Downey (Vice President Corporate Communications (BCA)) to tireless support from Yvonne Leach (Director of 787 Communications), Ken Morton (Communications Director Australia/New Zealand, The Boeing Company) and his PA, Emma Hodsdon.

Great support was received from Martin Johnson (Vice President, Communications, Rolls-Royce Plc), Mike Tod (Air New Zealand General Manager Public Affairs and Group Communications), Lori Gunter (Communications Specialist (BCA)), Lori Murphy (787 Communications), Jennifer German (787 Communications) and Michael Lombardi (Corporate Historian, The Boeing Company).

We would also like to thank Gail Warner and Lisa Bottle (Goodrich), Helene Cox and Sandra Fearon (GKN/Ultra Electronics), Pam Tvrdy and Nancy Welsh (Rockwell Collins), Peg Hashem (Hamilton Sundstrand), Jennifer Villarreal and Heather Cox (Smiths Aerospace) and Caroline Harris (Smiths Group plc).

Thanks also to Jim Stump, Deborah Kase and Rick Kennedy (General Electric), Mark Sullivan (Pratt & Whitney) and Annalie Brown (Rolls-Royce).

Additional support and material have been provided by: Harold Adams (Chief Designer (ret.) Douglas Aircraft Company), the late Don Hanson (former Vice President of Douglas Aircraft Company, Corporate Communications) and Patricia McGinnis (Boeing Historical Archives - Long Beach).

Special thanks to Juanita Franzi of Aero Illustrations for her input into the graphs and Kerry Coyle for her hours of style editing and suggestions.

Very special thanks to our families whose endless support and patience has made this book possible.

Left to right: Guy Norris, Christine Forbes Smith, Geoffrey Thomas and Mark Wagner

About the authors

Guy Norris is the US West Coast Editor of the weekly *Flight International* and the author of 14 books on aviation. He was named Aerospace Journalist of the Year in 1997 in the Best Systems and Technology Submission, in 2004 in Best Propulsion Submission and was joint winner in 2005 for the Best Regional Aircraft Submission. Guy has also twice been nominated for the Boeing Decade of Excellence Award and twice won the Aviation/Space Writers' Association award. He has appeared in numerous aviation television documentaries and has authored several aerospace educational projects including the interactive Aviation Knowledge Adventure CD-ROM and the aerospace section of the Encyclopedia of Science in Action published by McMillan. He lives in Southern California with Anna Ravelo and their children Chris, Daniel, Greg, Lia and Tom.

Geoffrey Thomas is the Senior Editor of the airline management journal *Air Transport World*. Geoffrey was previously SE-Asian Contributing Editor for *Aviation Week and Space Technology*. He was named Aerospace Journalist of the Year in the Best Systems and Technology Submission for 2002 and 2003, won Australasian Aviation Journalist of the Year awards for 2001 and 2002 and was runner-up in 2003. In all, Geoffrey has won 14 international and Australasian awards. He has appeared in several aviation investigative documentaries and is a regular commentator on Australian TV and radio. He is regularly published in *WA Business News, The Australian*, *Sunday Times* and *Australian Aviation* and was previously published in *The West Australian*, *Sydney Morning Herald*, and *The Age*. Geoffrey has co-written four books and lives in Perth, Australia with his two sons Christopher and Nicholas.

Mark Wagner (MRAeS) is a pilot and specialist aviation photographer. He works as a photographer for the international photo agency Aviation-Images.com as well as for aerospace, airline and advertising clients worldwide. This is his 26th aviation book as photographer/author and he has had over 2,000 magazine, book and brochure front cover pictures published since 1985 (including *Time, Air & Space, AOPA Pilot, Flight International* and *Air Transport World*) and has been chief photographer for *Flight International* magazine since 1990. He lives in London, UK, with wife Stephanie and son Henry.

Christine Forbes Smith (B.A. (Social Sciences) and B. App. Sci.) is regularly published in *WA Business News* and was previously published in *The West Australian* travel pages focusing on consumer issues as well as destinations. Christine also writes for *Airways* magazine and has authored four books on aviation and travel. Christine lives in Perth, Australia with her three sons, Alex, Simon and Mitchell.

Introduction

Albert Einstein, perhaps the greatest mind of our time, once said: "Not everything that can be counted counts and not everything that counts can be counted."

Building a new aircraft can never be counted in dollar terms. The numbers may add up on an accountant's spreadsheet but most aspects of building a successful commercial aircraft program, and the subsequent flow-on, cannot be counted.

The most widely sold piston-engine commercial aircraft in history, the DC-3, was built on a commitment for 20, made over the phone in 1934, between two close friends, Donald Douglas and American Airlines CEO Cyrus R. Smith. The flow-on from this program – which revolutionized air travel – built a dynasty that would last for decades.

Some 30 years later, in 1952, legendary Boeing President William (Bill) Allen invested $16 million in the 367-80 transport prototype. He had no orders, just a gut instinct that he could snare the lucrative US Air Force tanker business and steal a march on his competitors for a jet transport – if he had an aircraft flying.

Boeing not only snatched the lead but has dominated commercial aviation for more than four decades since.

Ten years on, Douglas, again on a gut feeling, launched that company's most successful jetliner, the DC-9, without an order, although there were some commitments in the wings.

Successful commercial aircraft programs are all about seizing the initiative with technical innovation that translates into promises of lower operating costs and greater creature comforts. Boeing did it again with the 747 launching the wide-body era and, in the early 1990s, with the incredibly successful 777 launched the "giant twin".

Like the DC-3, Vickers Viscount, 707, 747, A300 and 777, the 787 promises to be a game-changer. As with its famous predecessors, the 787 incorporates a host of new technologies that combine and set it apart from its competitors. Its true value to the airline operators will not be realised until the ultimate judges – the passengers – step aboard. No salesman can put a true value on this aspect nor can a competing salesman discount it. It just can't be counted – at least, not in simple numbers.

As well as telling the story so far, *Boeing 787 Dreamliner – Flying Redefined* also details how "game-changing" aircraft have significantly altered the course of, and ultimately improved, commercial aviation.

Technology's effect on aviation has been pervasive and the industry is littered with the wreckage of airlines and aircraft manufacturers that miscalculated or just did not fully understand what a pivotal role technology would play in driving down costs and improving the performance of aircraft.

This book looks in detail at how technology has been the main driver of the extraordinary development of commercial aviation.

The 787 brings together the phenomenal talents of Boeing and its merged companies, Douglas Aircraft Company and McDonnell Aircraft Company (which had previously merged in 1967) and North American Aviation, which had, also in 1967, become a component of North American Rockwell and Hughes Space & Communications and was recently renamed Boeing Satellite Systems.

But more than that, the 787 melds the talents of a host of aerospace manufacturers, suppliers and software companies around the globe – all absolute leaders in their disciplines and each one helping to push the boundaries of discovery every day.

We have employed US measurements (and spelling) as they are the standard in aviation. Boeing changed the name of its 787 from 7E7 in January 2005, however, for the sake of simplicity, we have altered the name to 787 much earlier in its history.

We sincerely hope that you enjoy *Boeing 787 Dreamliner – Flying Redefined* and we welcome your feedback.

Geoffrey Thomas, Guy Norris, Mark Wagner and Christine Forbes Smith

chapter 1
Magnificent Heritage

Most of the things worth doing in the world had been declared impossible before they were done.
— Louis D. Brandeis —

Left: A replica of the B&W 1 float plane poses with New Zealand's National Airways Corporation's first Boeing 737-200. *Air New Zealand*

Right: William Edward Boeing *Boeing Historical Archives*

Back to the future

William Edward Boeing told his staff at the fledgling Boeing Company "to let no new improvement in flying and flying equipment pass us by".

Adherence to this philosophy has kept the world's largest aerospace company at the cutting edge of technology since 15 July 1916.

To fully appreciate this drive for excellence, let's examine in the next two chapters the stirrings of passion that drove the forefathers of aviation to ever increasing heights – way beyond the constant technological challenges and never-ending competition. In many ways, although taking place in a different era with a new set of technological boundaries, the development and philosophy behind the 787 Dreamliner is similar to many of the cutting edge design breakthroughs in the last century of flight.

More powerful, economical and reliable engines, lower fuel burn, aerodynamic, material and electronic advances, and greater passenger comfort and amenities

have always been the benchmarks for progress in commercial aviation. With the 787, it is the extraordinary combination of these factors – all at once – that ensures that it will become another of the iconic airplanes that cement their name in history as game-changers.

As often happens through history, it is a single event – one which appears almost incidental at the time – that changes the course of lives. For Bill Boeing, that event was a Fourth of July celebration on Lake Washington in 1914.

A chance joy flight and Boeing was hooked. He was determined to learn to fly and began to dream of building better flying machines.

Boeing shared his passion with good friend and navy engineer George Conrad Westervelt. In 1915, they started building their own float planes, which they called B&W Model 1, in Boeing's boathouse. Westervelt was then posted back to the East Coast and Boeing completed the two aircraft in 1916.

On 15 July 1916, Boeing incorporated his airplane manufacturing business as the

Pacific Aero Products Company and, one year later, changed the name to Boeing Airplane Company.

The first Boeing sale was not to a US customer but to New Zealand. The two Boeing Model 1s purchased by the New Zealand Flying School were named Mallard and Bluebil. On 16 December 1919, the two aircraft operated the first New Zealand airmail service.

Boeing's foray into commercial transport was born out of the US Post Office mail contracts. The company won a mail contract with its Model 40 aircraft, which used a lighter air-cooled engine, giving the aircraft a 1,000lb and two passenger payload.

But Boeing was not content and strove to develop aircraft with better performance and comfort for passengers. Subsequently, the Model 80 took to the skies on 27 July 1928 – just 14 months after the Model 40.

The three-engine Model 80 carried 12 passengers and sported a heated cabin, leather seats, individual reading lamps and hot and cold running water. Boeing was already thinking of passengers' needs – and more was to come.

First around the world

Donald Wills Douglas (Don Douglas) often told his staff: "Dream no small dream, it lacks magic. Dream large. Then make the dream real." They were the driving words that ensured the Douglas Aircraft Company's lead in commercial aviation for decades.

And according to Walt Gillette, Vice President 787 Airplane Development, that Douglas influence of "making the dream real" can be found today in the design philosophy that makes up the 787. In his opinion, "the 787 is the first Boeing-Douglas aircraft".

For Don Douglas, the dream started when he saw Orville Wright perform the final test flights for US Army acceptance of the Wright Flyer and, according to Wilbur Morrison in his book, *A*

Heart with Wings, "Don was fascinated as the machine circled the field at speeds averaging 42 miles an hour."

Like Bill Boeing on the other side of the country, Douglas was overcome with emotion and determined to combine his love of the sea with his new passion. He resigned from the Naval Academy at Annapolis because he felt he was wasting his time building models of planes and entered the Massachusetts Institute of Technology (M.I.T.) to study engineering. Graduating in just two years, his first job was to help design M.I.T.'s first wind tunnel and to develop the aerodynamics and aeronautical engineering course.

A year later, in 1915, Douglas joined Glenn Martin's aircraft company as chief engineer and then, in 1917, undertook a brief stint as the US Army's first chief civilian aeronautical engineer. After World War I hostilities ended, he rejoined Martin and

designed the MB-1 bomber, the largest aircraft yet built for the US Army.

In March 1920, Douglas headed for Los Angeles to form his own company. With the help of local financier, David Davis, he built the Cloudster, which made its first flight in February 1921. The Cloudster was to start a Douglas tradition characterized by the pursuit of economy and ruggedness in design. It was the first airplane to lift a payload greater than its own weight. And the Cloudster formed the basis for the Douglas World Cruisers (DWC), which became the first aircraft to fly around the world in 1924.

Through the 1920s, the Douglas Aircraft Company slowly grew as a result of orders from the US Navy and the US Army for observation planes, as well as orders for mail planes, such as the M-1.

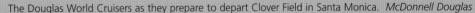

The Douglas World Cruisers as they prepare to depart Clover Field in Santa Monica. *McDonnell Douglas*

The DC-3 was the first aircraft that could make money just hauling passengers.
McDonnell Douglas

The plane that changed the world

America's newfound passion for travel and the advent of more powerful engines saw Boeing, and its associated airline companies, develop the Boeing 247, which was the world's first truly modern airliner.

As with the 787 today, Boeing seized all the latest technology and embodied it in the 247, which built on the design work of the six-passenger Model 221 Monomail – an airplane that first flew on 6 May 1930.

The 247 made its first flight in February 1933 and was a whopping 30 miles (48km) per hour faster than the Ford Tri-motor – the best aircraft to that date. Although nothing by today's standards, in 1933, the 247 cut four hours off the US transcontinental flying time, making the crossing in just 19 hours.

Even greater performances were on the way. United Airline's order for seventy-six 247s tied up Boeing's production lines and forced archrival Transcontinental and Western Airlines (TWA) to issue a request for the manufacture of an aircraft with tough specifications that would blitz the 247. Abiding by his

philosophy of "dreaming large and dreaming magic", Don Douglas responded and set his engineers to work.

TWA had set Douglas a demanding challenge for that time of building an aircraft that could carry 10 passengers at a top speed of 185mph (300kmh) to a range of 940nm (1,740km). The resulting prototype twin-engine DC-1 was a stunning success.

Douglas won the business but TWA's bankers baulked at lending the airline money to buy the slightly larger DC-2 because they were skeptical that such an aircraft could be built.

These new all-metal airliners were crammed with new technological and safety features – variable speed propellers, auto-pilot, powered brakes, wing flaps, retractable landing gear systems and duplicate instruments in the cockpit.

The extraordinary DC-3 evolved after American Airlines demanded a wider aircraft that could take sleeping berths. But it was in its daytime configuration of 21 passengers that the DC-3 excelled. It was the first aircraft that could make money just hauling passengers. By virtue of better streamlining, it had only marginally more drag than the DC-2, despite carrying 50% more passengers. Compared to the Ford Tri-motor, the DC-3 was 40% more fuel efficient, even though its speed had increased by almost 100%.

The DC-3 made all other aircraft obsolete overnight – so much so that by 1941, 80% of airliners on US domestic scheduled services were DC-3s. Airlines had to buy the DC-3 or face ruin.

Boeing and Douglas were now locked in battle to harness new technology to improve safety, passenger amenities and provide airlines with an economic edge.

Pressurization

The next battleground between Boeing and Douglas was a nil-all draw as World War II halted development of passenger planes. But valuable lessons were learnt that would serve to focus manufacturers on precisely what the industry demanded – economy and value, which are similarly the cornerstones of the 787.

Douglas flew its four-engine DC-4E on 7 June 1938 – incidentally, the same day as Boeing flew its magnificent 314 Clipper, which is covered on the next page.

The DC-4E was born out of a desire to fly across the US with just one stop but airlines rejected the proof-of-concept aircraft because its luxurious fittings added a great deal of weight and therefore expense. It featured a bridal suite, check-room for clothing and carry-on luggage, a ladies' lounge, which boasted "everything for milady's boudoir in spacious, elegant seclusion." The men were not forgotten with a men's dressing room with toilet, three washbasins and a couch.

A much leaner DC-4 was ordered by the airlines as they focused on eliminating the frills to get costs down.

Douglas had produced 21 of the first 61 DC-4s that were ordered when the bombing of Pearl Harbor saw the aircraft destined for United and American Airlines, commandeered by the US Army as troop transports. Eventually, Douglas built 1,241 DC-4s, mainly for the military.

In Seattle, Boeing went one step better, with its pressurized four-engine 307 Stratoliner airliner. The first flight was on 31 December 1938 but as war clouds gathered, only 10 were built. Four went to Pan American, five to TWA and one to Howard Hughes. The 307 could carry 32 passengers and fly at altitudes of 20,000ft (6,096m) – above most of the worst weather. TWA put the aircraft into service between Los Angeles and New York via Chicago in 1940.

The 307 was pressed into military colors in the war years as the C-75 but no more were ordered, with the military preferring the simpler DC-4 and the more potent C-69 Constellation from Lockheed.

After six years of restoration work by Boeing employees and retirees, an ex-Pan Am Boeing 307 "Clipper Flying Cloud" took to the air in 2001. Many Boeing suppliers donated parts and furnishings to bring the 307 back to her original glory. The aircraft is now displayed in the Steven F Udvar-Hazy Center at Washington Dulles International Airport, companion of the Smithsonian's National Air and Space Museum. *Joe Walker*

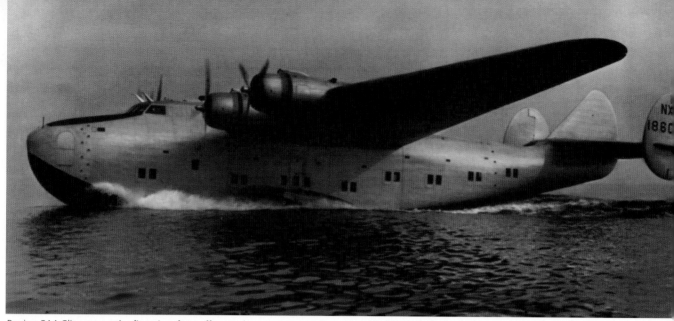

Boeing 314 Clipper was the first aircraft to offer regular passenger services across the North Atlantic. *Boeing Historical Archives*

Luxury on the water

Despite the lack of sales success, Boeing designs were at the forefront of technology and luxury.

The ultimate expression for its day was the Boeing 314 Clipper flying boat, which could carry an economic payload of 35 passengers across the Atlantic in either direction. It had a 14-seat dining room and sleeping berths for all passengers.

Key to its performance were the aircraft's four 1,550hp Wright Cyclone engines – the most powerful engines fitted to any pre-war aircraft. By comparison, the DC-3 engines were just 1,200hp.

By the end of the 1930s, piston engines had evolved from a post-war best of 400hp with an overhaul rate of 75 hours to 1,550hp engines with a six-fold improvement in overhaul rate. Of critical importance was the accompanying 50% decrease in engine weight per horsepower developed. More powerful engines also meant better speed.

The return fare across the Atlantic in those days was $675, equivalent to 20 weeks' salary at the time. The 314 had a 10-man flight crew and required a marathon inspection at the end of each flight. No fewer than 1,500 inspections had to be made by 200 men. The turnaround took six days when the service first started in 1939. This was later reduced to 48 hours.

The 314 was a magnificent aircraft by any standards. It could carry 74 passengers to 1,725nm (3,194km) or 35 on the much longer trans-Atlantic trip. However, the era of the flying boats was finished as more powerful engines enabled much more economical land planes to cross the vast oceans.

Passengers passed many hours in the dining room of the Boeing 314 clipper. *Boeing Historical Archives*

Tourist class soars

As war clouds began to clear, the US defense forces were scaling back on orders and all manufacturers turned to airlines for salvation. But that strategy was complicated by the huge numbers of surplus army transports that flooded the market.

Again, it was technology that was the answer to sales – just as it is today. Douglas flew its DC-6 in February 1946 and Lockheed's Constellation flew in 1943 under military guise.

The new planes harnessed the increase in reliability and performance of piston engines, which had soared through the war. In 1939, Boeing's 314 engines developed a respectable 1,550hp, but by war's end, the USAF B-36's Pratt & Whitney engines produced 3,500hp. At the same time, the engine's fuel consumption dropped, its weight was reduced and the time between overhauls almost doubled to 1,000 hours. By comparison, the time between overhauls requiring the complete removal of the engine from the wing today, can be as long as 40,000 hours over nine years – a record held by the Rolls-Royce RB211-535E4 fitted to a 757.

These improvements meant that from 1942, when the DC-4 first flew, to the final development of the family of aircraft known as the DC-7C in 1955, Douglas was able to double the payload, take-off weight and range as well as increase the speed by more than 50%.

These aircraft and Boeing's magnificent 377 Stratocruiser featured a host of innovations, such as hydraulic power-boosted controls and thermal de-icing. Additionally, the Constellation's sleek design translated into exceptional performance. Its top speed of 347mph (643kmh) was faster than any World War II bomber – and as fast as most fighters.

The widespread introduction of more economical four-engine land planes meant a substantial decline in costs for airlines. Between 1945 and 1950, Pan Am was able to bring fares down 30% and cargo rates had dropped by half. This led to the introduction of international tourist class in 1949 to San Juan and across the Atlantic in 1952.

It was an instant hit. Fares were 50% cheaper and traffic doubled within a year. By 1954, tourist class was available on all Pan Am routes and most routes around the world. Airlines and manufacturers were awakened to the enormous growth potential of air travel – when the price is right.

Air travel on board a DC-7C circa 1955 *McDonnell Douglas*

The Vickers Viscounts brought passengers turbine speed and magnificent panoramic windows. *BAE Systems*

The Viscount that would be king

Across the Atlantic, the turbine-powered Viscount built by Vickers Aircraft Company revolutionized air travel.

British European Airways (BEA), the state-owned domestic and European airline, needed a technological advantage to beat off competition from Air France and KLM, which were using profits from their long-haul routes to subsidize short-haul flights into London. That weapon was the 40-seat Viscount which BEA ordered in 1949.

The Viscount entered service in April 1953 on the London-Rome-Athens-Cyprus route for BEA and was an immediate success. Passengers loved the Viscount, which featured enormous oval picture windows affording a magnificent view. Only the 787 has windows of a similar size in the modern era.

The Viscount's Rolls-Royce turbine engines produced excellent speed and were virtually vibration-free. It was so well patronized that BEA was rated the fifth largest airline in the world judged on the number of passenger journeys made in 1960.

Its impact for BEA was extraordinary. The profits the airline made from operating the Viscount offset the losses by its other aircraft, putting BEA into profit. In 1960, the combined BEA Viscount fleet of 63 aircraft made £4 million ($7.5 million) profit on revenues of £32 million, at a time when BEA made £2 million over its entire operations. Aside from the first two years of its introduction, the Viscount kept BEA in profit every year until 1961.

The aircraft was so dominant that key European airlines – Air France, KLM and Lufthansa – all ordered it to compete with BEA.

In Australia, the story was similar, with the government-owned domestic airline, Trans Australia Airlines (TAA) ordering Viscounts while Australian National Airlines (ANA) opted for the larger but slower DC-6Bs. Passengers in Australia flocked to the Viscount and, as with the DC-3 20 years earlier, the Viscount was a game-changer. TAA's introduction of the Viscount was a major factor in the demise of ANA and its takeover by the fledgling Ansett Airways in 1957.

These game-changing aircraft have altered the course of commercial aviation, their pivotal innovations having cemented their names in history. Similarly, the 787 will become a modern-day icon for technological advances which will fundamentally change the course of commercial aviation history.

chapter2
The Jet Wars

*This is the most important aviation development since Lindbergh's flight. In one fell swoop, we have shrunken the earth.
– Juan Trippe, founder of Pan Am, on the introduction of jet aircraft and their downward effect on airfares –*

Boeing 707s for TWA, American Airlines and Continental Airlines at Renton, Seattle *Boeing Historical Archives*

The $16 million gamble

Donald Douglas Jnr said that "every major advance in aviation has been linked to the aircraft engine" and one of the major factors in the 787's compelling economics is its ultra-high bypass jet engines. But 64 years ago, the jet engine was an unreliable novelty, producing just 850lb of thrust. However, by the end of WWII, it had been developed into an awesome source of power for its day, producing 4,000lbs of thrust.

Britain's de Havilland Aircraft Company flew its Comet passenger jet in 1949 and in May 1950, Wellwood Beall – Vice President Engineering for the Boeing Aircraft Company – flew to England on the delivery flight of the last BOAC Stratocruiser. While in England, he saw the de Havilland Comet and recognized that the future of commercial aviation was in the jet-powered airliner. He also saw a great opportunity for Boeing to overcome Douglas' lead in airline aircraft sales. In a meeting in April 1952, he convinced the Boeing board.

At the same time, the US Air Force (USAF) was talking about a military tanker to replace its KC-97 tanker. Boeing's President Bill Allen had plenty of the "right stuff" and was prepared to back his judgment and that of his chief engineer. They committed $16 million on a jet transport prototype to help secure the USAF tanker order. The promise of jet-powered transport was irresistible, offering almost double the speed and payload for 22% less cost per seat than the best piston-engine aircraft of the day, the DC-6B.

The Boeing 367-80 prototype of the 707 which resulted and the Douglas DC-8 which followed went on to dominate commercial aviation. Although they had price tags double that of the piston-engine aircraft they would replace, they produced three times the revenue.

When the 707 entered service with Pan Am in 1959, there was a scramble to get a seat, with the airline's flights running at an extraordinary 90.8% load factor. Passengers loved the jets. In the first five years of jet operations, Pan Am's overseas traffic doubled.

In 1960, for the first time, the number of passengers crossing the North Atlantic by air topped those on ocean liners. Pan Am was offering a return trip across the North Atlantic from only $298 – just slightly above what the one-way fare had been in 1952 – or just three weeks' average salary in the US.

Not only were fares plummeting – so were traveling times. Australia's Qantas was able to slash the London-Sydney route from 48 hours to 27 hours. Airlines now had aircraft that had caught the public's imagination.

In the modern era, analysts and airline management personnel again believe that Boeing's 787 will fire the public's imagination. Like its predecessors, the 787's development has required the commitment and fortitude of the manufacturer's management team.

The impossible jets

While the promise of jet power was immense, Boeing realized that something extra was needed to access many of the airports with shorter runways.

The 727 Design Team Conference (*Left to Right*): Pfafman, controls; Maxam, systems; Sutter, technology; Steiner, Chief Project Engineer; Watney, structures and Norton, aerodynamics. *Boeing Historical Archives*

In February 1956, Boeing launched its 727 project, which was deemed "mission impossible" by a host of nay-sayers, in the same way that critics today have labeled the 787 too advanced. The aim in 1956 was to carry 131 passengers from a 5,000ft long airfield, which was the typical length of most of the smaller airports. At the same time, BEA issued a less demanding specification for an aircraft that could operate into a 6,000ft (1,829m) runway and carry 100 economy class passengers up to 1,200nm (2,222km). What evolved was a radical three-engine aircraft with a T-tail and BEA ordered the de Havilland Trident in August 1959.

But for Boeing engineers, the challenge of convincing the board that there was a market for the medium-range 727, which was smaller than the 707, was a major hurdle – almost as great as designing the jet. Key launch airlines, such as American,

Eastern, TWA and Delta, had ordered either four-engine turboprop Lockheed Electras or four-engine Convair CV880 jets for shorter ranges. Boeing was late into this market.

However, Boeing's engineers, such as the legendary Jack Steiner and Joe Sutter, were convinced they could design a much better machine than the competition. They were determined to carry through Bill Boeing's policy of "letting no technical achievement pass us by".

Airlines wanted more cruise speed but slower landing speeds. The solution was found in a unique wing design that colorful Trans Australia Airlines' Chief Engineer John Maskiell described in amazement and with a wry smile as the "wing that comes apart".

And on landing, come apart it did. On the trailing edge of the wing were massive triple-slotted flaps totaling 388sq ft with a 40°

setting. These were combined with leading edge slats on the entire length of the wing plus seven spoilers on each wing – typical today but unique in 1962. When the 727 flew on 9 February 1962, it was off the ground in just 3,000ft (914m) and landed in an incredible 2,000ft (610m).

The 727's stunning performance sounded the death knell for a number of designs, such as the Lockheed Electra and Convair 880 and 990. Jet-engine performance improvements, combined with advances in aerodynamics, meant that, for the first time in aviation, a three-engine jet could perform the same mission as a four-engine model. The 727 and the Trident were landmark designs.

The message was clear once again – technology used wisely, would obsolete aircraft overnight – a message that was well to the fore as the 787 began to take shape.

American Airlines Boeing 727-100 *Boeing Historical Archives*

Dual production lines struggle to meet demand for the DC-9 twin-jets. The scene was similar for the Boeing 737.
McDonnell Douglas

Twin-jets take off

Today we take twin-jet travel across vast oceans for granted but in the early 1960s a twin-jet aircraft was treated with extreme caution. But just as the reliability of jet engines and aerodynamic technology gave rise to the development of the 727 and Trident, it also made possible the successful development of the twin-jet.

The twin-jet came first in the form of the Caravelle designed by Sud Aviation, one of the forerunners of Airbus Industrie. The Caravelle flew on 27 May 1955 from Toulouse. British Aircraft Corporation launched its 1-11 in 1961 and Douglas committed to its DC-9 in 1963.

The economics of twin-jets were so compelling that Boeing could not resist entering the market, despite starting a very distant fourth among its competitors. American and Braniff had ordered the 1-11 and archrival Douglas had sown up Delta, Eastern and TWA. Of the "majors", only United was left. It was, however, the European "major" Lufthansa that first ordered the newly developed 737.

In what can only be described as the greatest success story in jet aviation, the 737 has outlived all its competitors and sales had topped 5,808 by June 30, 2005.

The secret to the 737's success has been an aggressive program of updating the aircraft to keep pace with the latest technology. The latest model the -900ER has an 85% range increase, 117% greater passenger load at 133% lower seat mile costs than the first 737.

That performance has been matched by a dramatic increase in technology in the cockpit and airplane safety systems. The first 737s had an accident rate of 1.26 accidents per one million departures and the latest New Generation model has an unblemished safety record.

With Airbus' extremely successful A320 series, the single-aisle twin-jets continue to dominate commercial aviation, linking countless city pairs around the globe and crossing oceans, such as the Atlantic, every day with ease.

Donald Douglas Jnr, Donald Douglas Snr with GM Aircraft Division Jackson McGowan at the roll-out of the first DC-9. *McDonnell Douglas*

Supersonic sidestep

The foray into supersonic travel was a painful lesson for the industry and for governments. It illustrated that economics is the most significant driver in aviation and that national pride and government meddling have no place in setting the agenda for commercial aviation.

In November 1962, the French and British governments signed off on a joint supersonic transport (SST) called the Concorde and Russia joined the race a year later. Incredibly, the French and British governments made no provision for a ceiling on costs (estimated to be £170 million), nor were review or cancellation processes agreed – except that whoever cancelled would have to repay the other government's entire funding costs.

Pan Am's long-time adviser, the famous Charles Lindbergh, warned of the environmental and economic problems the aircraft would face. But Britain saw the SST as its entry ticket to the Common Market.

Concorde's costs climbed faster than the superjet and, according to one estimate from the London-based *Independent* newspaper in 2003, the total write-off for the British and French governments was eventually $23.4 billion in today's dollars, which works out to a taxpayer subsidy of a staggering $5,500 for every passenger who has flown on Concorde.

Boeing established a supersonic project office in January 1958 but, because of the enormous cost of the project, it was rightly thought to be beyond the fiscal capability of any private company. Despite doubts, and possibly because of airline orders for Concordes, President John F. Kennedy launched the US counter to the Concorde.

Boeing won the race with its swing wing 2707-200 and 26 airlines reserved 122 delivery positions. But the swing wing proved too great a technological hurdle. Despite a revised delta wing aircraft, the program was scrapped by Congress in 1971 on justifiable economic and environmental concerns.

The supersonic folly was clearly the result of unrealistic assessments by governments and industry of the viability of the market for such aircraft. The facts are sobering:

- The Concorde burnt one ton of fuel for every passenger carried across the North Atlantic.
- The Concorde fare across the North Atlantic was up to 30 times higher than the cheapest economy fare.

- None of the combined 37 SSTs built was ever purchased by an airline in real terms.
- All had massive development costs.
- All had enormous environmental problems related to the sonic boom.

Noted industry historian R.E.G. Davies pointed out in *Airways* in 1995 that little research was ever done into the market for SSTs. According to Davies, British Aircraft Corporation produced a brochure in 1970 claiming that more than 30% of the market would pay first class fares to travel on Concorde. He noted that in reality only 7% of the market was first class and that it was declining. In 2005 it was less than 2%, with many airlines dropping first class altogether on the North Atlantic.

The industry's brief flirtation with speed was a sobering lesson that advances in technology in pursuit of greater speed and size must at all times be tempered by the economic reality of what passengers are prepared to pay for such factors.

When Boeing proposed the near-supersonic Sonic Cruiser in 2000, airlines were initially lured by the speed but when they saw the economic gains from the same technology being applied to a conventional design, they were sold on what became the 787.

Four Concordes in formation for a media photo shoot
British Airways

Left: The first 747 poses with stewardesses from the airlines that had purchased the giant jet in 1968. *Boeing Historical Archives*
Right: The father of the 747 Joe Sutter (right) poses with John Travolta, movie star, aviation enthusiast and Qantas' "Ambassador at Large" and current President and CEO of Boeing Commercial Airplanes, Alan Mulally. *Geoffrey Thomas*

The jumbo era

In stark contrast to the hugely expensive supersonic aircraft, the jumbo era brought about huge cost savings and reduced airfares considerably.

The larger aircraft were possible because of the development of the big fan-jet for the USAF heavy lift aircraft, the C-5.

General Electric's (GE) TF-39 engine would produce 41,000lb of thrust – 125% more than the turbofan engines powering the 707-320 – and burn 25% less fuel.

Lockheed and GE eventually won the battle for the C-5 contract. Boeing and Pratt & Whitney (P&W) turned to civil applications and on 13 April 1966, Pan Am ordered 25 747s. The 747 was expected to cut operating costs by 30% over the 707. Other airlines reluctantly followed but their orders were limited to just a few to stay competitive as Douglas and Lockheed touted smaller jumbos powered by three engines.

Despite many problems encountered in its manufacture, the birth of the 747 was an amazing feat. Pan Am took delivery of its first aircraft just 3 years after its order was placed and that included a 10-month flight-test program. But Boeing was wounded. It owed $19 billion in 2005 dollars and had to lay off 64,000 staff to survive as business slumped. That business went south to Lockheed and the newly merged McDonnell Douglas Corporation (MDC) with their L-1011 and DC-10 tri-jets, which were far better suited to the market and city pairs.

These tri-jets resulted from an American Airlines' requirement for a 250-seat twin-jet to fly out of New York's La Guardia airport with its shorter runways. But many US airlines wanted transcontinental range and were also leery about operating twin-jets over the Rocky Mountains. The extraordinary reliability of the big jet engines was yet to be proven.

Another lesson was about to be learnt as MDC and Lockheed slugged it out over a market not sufficient to support two designs.

Responding to the same American Airlines' specification, France, Germany and Britain agreed in 1966 to cooperate on the Airbus project. By April of the next year, government funds were flowing to the project team, which resulted in the outstanding twin-engine 250-seat A300.

While, technically, Airbus had struck the right formula, sales did not flow immediately and it was not until the mid-1970s that airlines were taking notice of the economics of the "big twin" that Airbus pioneered.

Twin engines dominate

By the mid-70s, the large turbofan engine proved to be incredibly reliable. And that reliability meant maintenance costs were plummeting.

Airbus led the way with its A300, with the big three US manufacturers still recovering from the massive development costs of their three and four-engine jumbo jets.

Boeing made yet another bold decision and launched the twin-aisle 234-seat 767 and the single-aisle 200-seat 757 in 1978. Airbus responded with a smaller version of its A300, dubbed the A310.

Both Boeing and Airbus strove to expand the markets for the new twin-jets with trans-oceanic capability which opened the doors to a flood of orders. By the late 1970s, jets exhibited a 10-fold improvement in reliability over piston-engine aircraft. Thus, the Federal Aviation Authority (FAA) moved to ease the 60-minute rule to 120 minutes for twin-engine aircraft.

This was introduced in 1985 under a program called Extended-Range Twin Engine Operations (ETOPS). To get ETOPS approval, an airline had to demonstrate 12 months of satisfactory operation to agreed standards with an aircraft/engine combination that had an In-flight Shutdown (IFSD) rate of 0.05/1,000 hours or better.

Regulators were aware even then that engine reliability was only a small factor and ETOPS-certified aircraft had to have additional safety features, including:

- Additional cooling monitoring
- Extra back-up hydraulic motor/generator
- Revised Engine Instrument Crew Alerting System (EICAS)
- Increased Auxiliary Power Unit reliability with higher-altitude starting capability
- Additional cargo compartment fire suppression
- Duplicate electrical system

To meet the more stringent requirements, Boeing and Airbus had to add capability and modify their current designs. Later, aircraft such as the 777 were designed from the outset to be ETOPS-compliant.

The first ETOPS flight was on 1 February 1985 when a TWA Boeing 767-200 flew 2,986nm from Boston to Paris. Within 10 years, this was the most widely used transport across the North Atlantic. Today, 96% of aircraft crossing the North Atlantic are twin-engine.

Airlines such as Air New Zealand and Qantas also were to the fore with ETOPS. They soon operated their 767s around the Pacific on routes such as Auckland-Honolulu. Air New Zealand was the first airline to achieve 180-minutes ETOPS in 1989.

Twin-engine aircraft were now accepted as extremely reliable – in fact, more reliable than four and three-engine aircraft because of the additional back-up systems on board. The vast operational and design experience gained in ETOPS was incorporated into the 777 and the A330 (covered on page 22), the 787 and the A350.

Air New Zealand 767-300ER eats up the miles on yet another ETOPS flight.
Air New Zealand

The giant twins

Through the 1980s, Airbus and MDC developed new larger models of their existing designs – the A300 and the DC-10 – based on the guarantee of increased power from engine manufacturers. MDC launched its upgrade of the three-engine DC-10, the MD-11, in late 1986 and Airbus followed with its medium-range A330 and long-range four-engine A340 in 1987 using a common wing to save on development costs. Efforts to merge the two giants failed in 1988.

Beoing 777-300ER touches down at Perth, Western Australia as a part of its certification program. *Geoffrey Thomas*

Boeing watched and waited as even bigger engine growth was on the horizon. In 1991, despite the fact that the Airbus and MDC designs had captured the lion's share of the market, Boeing moved with its clean-sheet 777. As with the A330, the 777 was designed at the outset to be ETOPS compliant.

The Boeing 777 was an instant success and many airlines that had ordered the MD-11, such as American, Delta and KLM, swapped to the 777. In fact, Singapore Airlines dumped its MD-11s because of a range shortfall in favor of the A340-300 and then eventually disposed of them in favor of the 777-200ER.

Not to be denied, Airbus responded to the 777 threat in two ways: by redesigning the wing of its

A340 and by adding larger Rolls-Royce engines. Boeing countered by introducing the more powerful 777-300ER and -200LR, which have chalked up significant sales.

As the industry entered the 21st century, it was clear that regional commercial aviation would be dominated by single-aisle twin-engine short-haul aircraft, while the big twins of varying sizes would command the lion's share of the twin-aisle long-haul market because of their compelling economics.

The 787 was born from this experience and holds even greater promise of unmatched reliability with engine makers Rolls-Royce and General Electric confidently predicting that their engines for the 787 will have zero shutdowns.

The best way to predict the future is to invent it.
– Alan Kay –

Pan Am Boeing 377 Stratoliner
Boeing Historical Archives

It's a long way to London

In the previous two chapters, we traced the major technological advances in aviation, which led to the design philosophy of the 787. But to understand how airlines will use the 787's breakthrough technology, we need to examine the way markets have evolved and how they are changing.

One of the most hotly debated issues is whether passengers will demand more non-stops or continue to accept flights through hubs. Some may suggest that the marketing hype for non-stops, like the dot.com companies, is a recent phenomenon but history shows that the demand has always been there. The handicaps have been the lack of range of aircraft, the small markets in times past, as well as restricted market access.

It seems incredible today, as we book a non-stop flight from Phoenix to London on a British Airways 777-200ER, that 55 years ago it was a journey of epic proportions governed by the economic range of the piston-engine aircraft of the day.

First stage was to fly from Phoenix to San Francisco in a DC-3 to join an American Airlines DC-6 to New York, where passengers would transfer to a Pan American Boeing 377. Then it was a short hop to Stephenville in Newfoundland, Canada, for fuel before the flight across the Atlantic to Dublin, which was close to the limit of the 377's range with an economic payload. Final leg was to London. Today, there are just over 650 weekly non-stops from 21 US cities to London – up 170% since 1978.

On the other side of the world, Australia's Qantas chose the 377's competitor, the Lockheed Constellation, as its flagship and the trip to London was even more convoluted. The airline's first Constellation service – a weekly flight to London – was launched on 1 December 1947. The flight stopped at Darwin before overnighting in Singapore. The next day it was Calcutta, then Karachi, before flying on to Cairo. On the final day, it was on to London via Tripoli and Rome (see graph page 29).

Not only was range a problem but the airfares were so high that the traffic did not support direct services to most cities. The fare in the early 1950s from Sydney to London return was the equivalent of 55 weeks' average weekly earnings.

Cities such as London, Los Angeles, New York and Sydney – often headquarters for major airlines – evolved as hubs to funnel passengers on to trans-oceanic flights in big aircraft that could carry the large amount of fuel required to cross oceans.

An extreme example of the number of stops required was the London to Cape Town, South Africa service in the 1930s. Imperial Airways started regular air services in January 1932 from London to Cape Town. This remarkable journey took 11 days, 32 stops, five different aircraft and two train trips – the passengers would have loved a non-stop!

Seven Seas

The demand for non-stops was illustrated in 1951, when American Airlines CEO Cyrus Smith pressured the Douglas Aircraft Company into building an aircraft that could fly from New York to the US west coast non-stop against the headwinds. American was quick to advertise DC-7 non-stops with full-page advertisements in such newspapers as the *New York Times*.

Pan American wanted even more range to cross the Atlantic non-stop in a westerly direction and the DC-7C – which had a larger wing to hold more fuel – was ordered in July 1954.

The DC-7C, with its additional range – double that of the DC-6B – eliminated the number of refueling stops required. Airlines scrambled to buy the DC-7C and the L1649 Constellation to offer these non-stop options despite the fact that jets were only two years away, such was the demand for speed and fewer refueling stops.

The marketing power of the DC-7C, which became known as "The Seven Seas", was so remarkable that British Overseas Airways Corporation (BOAC) was forced to buy DC-7Cs when it learnt that the

Britannias, which it had ordered for the same mission, would be delayed by a year. Non-stops, even in 1957, were critical to airline success.

However, the DC-7C's range of 3,135nm (5,810km) with a full payload, meant that it had to shed some payload to make the 3,451nm from London to New York. A more potent power source was needed to connect the world.

American Airlines advertisement touting the first non-stop flights from New York to Los Angeles.

The need to match competition to provide non-stop services prompted BOAC to order 10 Douglas DC-7Cs.
McDonnell Douglas

Jets for restless wings

Jets had held enormous promise for years but high fuel burn and noise issues were of deep concern. At the same time, piston engines had become less reliable as their power had increased.

In fact, they had become so twitchy that the DC-7C suffered one engine failure every 158 flights compared to one every 450 flights on the DC-6B.

After a tragic false start, marred by structural failure of the Comet 1s, BOAC ordered 19 of the greatly improved and structurally stronger Comet 4s in February 1955. First customer to announce its intention to order US-built jets was not Pan Am, as is often quoted, but Miami-based National Airlines, which declared its order for six DC-8s in August 1955. The pivotal buy, however, was Pan Am's famous announcement for 25 DC-8s and 20 707s on 13 October 1955.

Jets were game-changers, just as the DC-3 and pressurization had been. Regardless of how many piston-engine aircraft airlines had, jets were absolutely crucial or they would be ruined. So much so that within seven years, airlines had taken delivery of 666 DC-8s, 707s, 720s, CV880s, CV990s and Caravelles and had ordered hundreds of 727s, VC-10s, Tridents and BAC 1-11s.

Aside from their speed and economy, jets were virtually vibration-free and enabled aircraft to soar well above the worst of the weather. Travel was now a real pleasure – and not nearly as painful on the wallet. According to the Air Transport Association of America (ATA), the economy and popularity of jets saw traffic soar in the US through the 1960s by a whopping 172% – a growth rate that has never been repeated.

Jets were irresistible, blitzing all other aircraft then in service. The 707's and DC-8's performances were a quantum leap and, although they cost double that of

piston-engine aircraft, they produced three times the revenue. That productivity was put into context in Ray Whitford's comprehensive series, *Fundamentals of Airliner Design* published in *Air International*. Whitford found that airliner productivity had risen from a base of zero in 1920 to 20 by 1955 with the DC-7C. The 707's index was 60 and the longer-range 707-320C took that index to 125.

For passengers, that translated into much lower airfares and Australians and New Zealanders found that they could fly to London for just 20 weeks' salary compared to 55 weeks on the piston-engine Constellation.

Importantly, jets offered airlines far greater range. The Douglas DC-8 Super 62 had a range of 5,210nm (9,620km) – 66% greater than the DC-7C. From London, it could over-fly New York and reach Los Angeles – or any destination in the USA – with a full payload. New York's status as a hub was starting to wane.

Final production being completed at Douglas on DC-8s for Pan American Airways, United Airlines, Delta Airlines and Air Canada. *McDonnell Douglas*

MDC came close to launching the DC-10 Twin in 1972. *McDonnell Douglas*

Reliability frees aerospace engineers

But the real potential of jet power was yet to be realized as the reliability of jets took time to register with airline executives, whose memories were still filled with the tragic consequences of piston-engine unreliability.

From 1945 to 1960, 117 twin-engine and 61 four-engine accidents were related to engine failures. Responding to those serious concerns, aircraft manufacturers around the world at the time held strongly to the view that "more is better" – even when it came to the number of jet engines.

But in the constant battle for competitive advantage, forward-thinking aircraft manufacturers quickly responded to the incredible reliability of jet engines once the 707 took to the air. Time between overhauls soared and in-flight shut down (IFSD) rates plummeted.

Douglas' DC-9, which originally had four engines, was scrapped in favor of a twin-engine model and Boeing built a three-engine 727 to do battle with the four-engine Convair 880. It was not long before engine growth and reliability enabled twin-engine aircraft such as the 737, DC-9/MD-80 and A320 to replace three-engine 727s and Tridents.

By the late 1970s, the future of aircraft design was clear. Twin-engine aircraft would dominate. It is interesting to note that Airbus and Boeing with their focus on twin-engine designs have survived, whereas McDonnell Douglas Corporation (MDC) and Lockheed with their tri-jet focus have exited the civil market. MDC came close in 1972 to launching the DC-10 Twin. Former president of the Douglas division, Jackson McGowan, lamented in an October 2004 interview: "We [MDC] missed the big twin."

The jet-engine reliability numbers are extraordinary. The IFSD rate has dropped from 0.9 shutdowns per 1,000 engine hours for the first turbojets on the 707/DC-8/Comet 4 to an incredible 0.005 shutdowns per 1,000 hours today. In fact, the GE90-115B engines on the 777-300ER (Extended Range) have recorded no shutdowns in more than a year of service as this book goes to press.

Rolls-Royce provides a fascinating insight into the effect of this improved reliability on airline bottom lines. It says that 20 years ago, the cost of the replacement parts and maintenance of an engine on a DC-10, would equal its original purchase price within eight years. Today, it takes 30 years for a 777 engine. That level of reliability has made the design layout of two engines for the 787 a formality.

And with a twin-engine layout, aerospace engineers can design more economical and efficient aircraft giving airlines far greater flexibility to match aircraft to route densities.

ETOPS eased and expanded

The increase in reliability for twin-engine aircraft certified for ETOPS (detailed on page 21), has been so profound that Airbus elected to certify its four-engine A340-500/600 to ETOPS standards to improve reliability.

A good example of the impact of strict ETOPS requirements on aircraft reliability was demonstrated when Boeing designed the 777 to achieve "out of the box" ETOPS status. It drew on the ETOPS experience with its 767s, made 160 refinements to the engine systems, 300 design modifications unrelated to the engines and dramatically improved reliability.

ETOPS was expanded from 180 minutes to 207 minutes after exhaustive industry study involving all interested parties including safety regulators. Regulators are also close to sanctioning 240-minute ETOPS and possibly beyond to 330-minutes with conditions.

Setting the tone for the new limits, the US regulator, the FAA, indicated when it issued its draft rule-making in January 2004, that engine reliability was

at such a high level that it was no longer a sufficiently significant issue to require limiting the allowed time from an airport.

The new ETOPS rules, based on the extraordinary reliability of aircraft today, virtually frees all twin-engine aircraft to fly any route required by the airlines.

Possibly the best perspective on the ETOPS debate, and what the incredible reliability of engines means, comes from Airbus which authored *ETOPS Twins Through Time* in 1989.

In the booklet, Airbus pointed out that in 1988, an ETOPS-equipped Airbus aircraft would have to fly back in time 8,940 years under 180-minute diversion criteria, before it suffered dual engine failure from independent causes. That is when the Sahara Desert was lush grassland!

And under the 120-minute diversion criteria, the aircraft would have to fly 17,880 years – back to the Ice Age. Those numbers were calculated when IFSD rates were 0.02/1,000 hours. Today, the 777 and A300-200 are demonstrating a rate of 0.005/1,000 hours.

Development of Non-Stop Markets

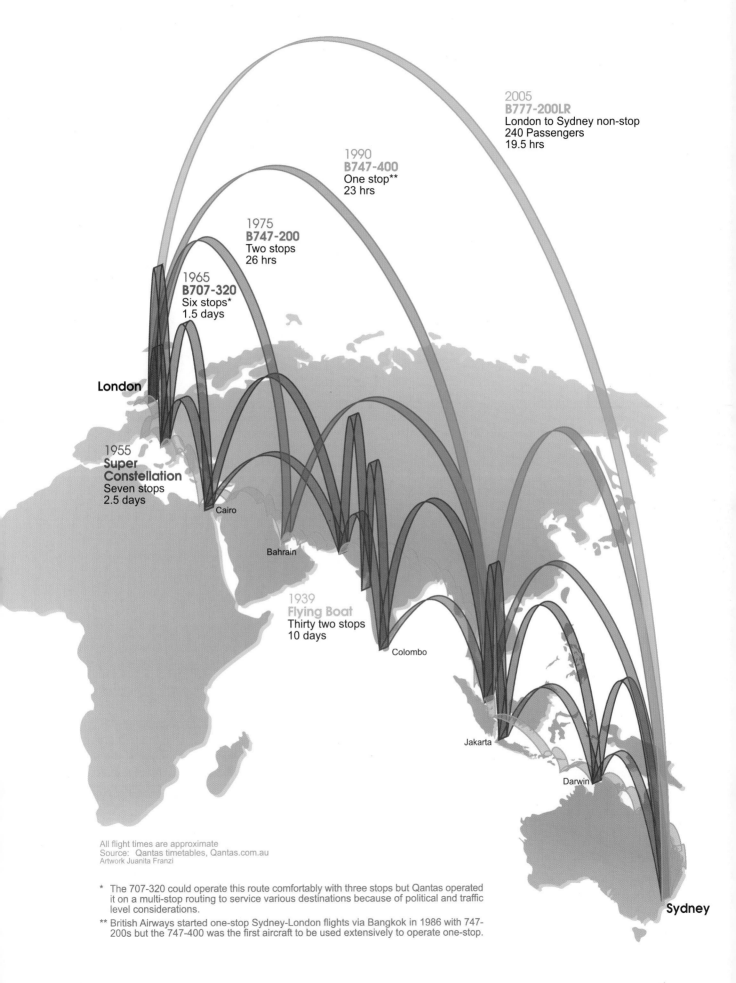

2005
B777-200LR
London to Sydney non-stop
240 Passengers
19.5 hrs

1990
B747-400
One stop**
23 hrs

1975
B747-200
Two stops
26 hrs

1965
B707-320
Six stops*
1.5 days

London

1955
**Super
Constellation**
Seven stops
2.5 days

Cairo

Bahrain

1939
Flying Boat
Thirty two stops
10 days

Colombo

Jakarta

Darwin

Sydney

All flight times are approximate
Source: Qantas timetables, Qantas.com.au
Artwork Juanita Franzi

* The 707-320 could operate this route comfortably with three stops but Qantas operated
   it on a multi-stop routing to service various destinations because of political and traffic
   level considerations.

** British Airways started one-stop Sydney-London flights via Bangkok in 1986 with 747-
   200s but the 747-400 was the first aircraft to be used extensively to operate one-stop.

The 777-200LR will enter service next year and is capable of carrying 240 passengers from London to Sydney Australia non-stop. *Boeing*

The hub-busters

With more economical twin-engine aircraft – freed of regulations that had their origins in the 1950s with piston-engine aircraft – airlines are able to meet market forces in innovative and flexible ways.

This has been demonstrated by the runaway sales of the A330 and 777 families for longer-range inter-continental operations. The 777 is the world's fastest selling wide-body with 702 sold between 1991 and mid-2005. The 787 is set to eclipse that record.

The 777, which carries between 300 and 365 passengers economically depending on the model, suits most major city pairs, such as Dallas-Tokyo and New York-Hong Kong.

The 787, and the proposed A350, will give airlines even more options and the versatility to bypass hubs by economically flying long ranges with smaller payloads, thereby opening up direct services between hundreds of smaller cities around the globe.

According to Mike Bair, Vice President 787 Program, the 787-8 will have a range capability to open up many new city pairs such as London-Perth, Seattle-Singapore, Adelaide-Los Angeles, Toronto-Guangzhou and Helsinki-Nanjing.

Some argue that travel demand between these smaller city pairs could be met quite adequately by three flights per week with larger aircraft. However, this ignores the fact that business travelers particularly, demand at least daily frequencies and are prepared to pay for it – a fact which underpins the economic reality of commercial aviation.

Qantas, which has ordered the giant 555-seat A380 has also joined the chorus, singing the hub-buster tune. In February 2004, Chief Financial Officer Peter Gregg told media that the airline was on the prowl for a hub-buster and was looking at offerings from Airbus and Boeing to "bypass hubs and offer passengers more non-stops". The Australian airline has long sought a "magic carpet" to carry passengers from London to Sydney non-stop.

chapter 4

Meeting Future Demand

Oh well, I suppose lots of people will do it now.
– Arthur Whitten Brown, to Captain John Alcock after
completing the first trans-Atlantic flight, 1919 –

737s line up for take-off. *Boeing*

Airlines - the life blood of economies

Like telephone lines, TV and satellites, airlines have become a vital and ever growing part of the global economy. In 2004, just over 1.8 billion passengers and 40%, by value, of the world's manufactured exports were moved by air, according to International Air Transport Association (IATA) figures.

The numbers are extraordinary and they are growing at an average of 5% annually, despite disasters such as 9/11 and the SARS epidemic.

A 2000 report on the *Economic Benefits of Air Transport* reveals that, since the first jetliner flew in 1949, air travel has grown 70-fold. And in 2000, there were over 18,000 aircraft operating into and out of 10,000 airports.

According to *Official Airline Guide (OAG)* figures, the growth of cities connected by air, dubbed city pairs, is relentless. For routes with jets over 100 seats, the number of city pairs climbed from 5,700 in 1985 to over 10,400 in 2004. For example, according to Eclat Consulting, between 1994 and 2002, US-based Southwest Airlines added 188 new city pairs, AirTran 82 and Frontier Airlines 31.

The latest generation of aircraft, which bring operating costs to new lows, are vital to help airlines meet the increasing demand for both travel and lower fares. And that demand is extraordinary in countries such as China, which has evolved into the world's second biggest economy.

Just 25 years ago, there were a total of 180 air routes in China (18 international) and only 3.43 million passengers took to the vacant skies each year. Incredibly, in 2004, China overtook Japan as the largest air travel market in Asia and is second only to the US in terms of total scheduled departing seats.

In the year 2004, passenger traffic soared 38% to 120 million passengers and cargo/mail carriage climbed 24.5% to 2.7 million tons.

Reflecting the massive growth and maturity of the China market, the country's major airlines have, for the first time, launched an airliner with the order for 60 787s placed in January 2005 and China Southern Airlines also ordered five A380s early in 2005.

The story is the same in India, where Air Deccan's Managing Director "GR" Gopinath said the potential market is incredible. "If growth continues, the current 600 flights a day (in India) will be 10,000 in ten years," he predicted.

And like the Chinese airlines, Air India has also – for the first time ever – helped launched a new aircraft with its order for 787-8s, announced in late April 2005.

According to Airbus' comprehensive *Global Market Forecast 2004-2023*, "while every US citizen on average makes 2.2 trips per year, the corresponding figures are just 0.02 trips per year in India and 0.06 in China." Airbus predicts that the combined purchasing power of India and China could be five times greater than the USA within 25 years.

The role of hubs

Naturally, as the market grows in size, more cities will be connected, either directly or through hubs. While passengers may wish to go non-stop, sometimes it is more practical to route passengers through hubs.

Hubs have evolved for a number of important reasons:

- They act as a consolidation point for passengers from much smaller cities so a wider range of city pair services can be offered to those passengers.
- Historically, aircraft did not have the range to allow non-stops between many destinations.
- Airlines used hubs – usually their home base – to control traffic, particularly in the US.
- Sometimes use of larger aircraft through hubs can reduce fares, depending on landing charges, taxes and congestion.
- Both domestic and international markets were regulated preventing airlines from starting new services.

Hubs developed to a high level in the US after deregulation in 1979, when airlines were suddenly free to serve any city, in stark contrast to the previously protracted process of gaining approvals. American Airlines led the charge and its competitors quickly followed to snare as much traffic as possible.

But traveling via hubs was not necessarily what passengers wanted. One of the major problems for hubs is that as they get bigger, the connections become more difficult with more delays likely as passengers become lost and miss their connections. Also, the often touted cost benefits of using larger aircraft through hubs reduces as the significant landing costs associated with major hubs are undercut by regional airports.

In March 2004, landing a 747-400 at Japan's Narita Airport cost $8,952 compared to just $420 for landing a 737-800 at Perth, Western Australia.

According to highly respected industry author Professor Nawal Taneja, in his latest book *FASTEN YOUR SEAT BELT: The Customer is Flying the Plane* (Ashgate), major US airlines are starting to abandon their traditional hub models to win traffic back. Taneja said that some airlines are closing hubs and redesigning others to smooth out peaks and troughs in schedules.

The success of a hub often depends upon its location. A case in point is Dubai, which has evolved as a gateway to the Middle-East because of its more tolerant western-style laws, and as a focal point for traffic to Europe from Australasia as aircraft to date have not had the range to fly from Australia to Europe non-stop. As the illustration on page 34 shows, it has only been since 2002 with the arrival of the A340-500, and 2006 with the 777-200LR that aircraft have had the range to bypass hubs such as Dubai.

Dubai, and its airline Emirates, have built up a very effective hub by offering passengers a host of non-stop connections to major cities, such as London and five other less prominent cities in the UK. In the fifteen years since 1990, Emirates has increased its non-stop destinations from 30 to over 60.

Another airport that has been at the limit of aircraft range is Tokyo's Narita Airport, which is dealt with in more detail on page 36. It evolved as a hub more as a result of its geographical location between the US and China/SE-Asia than its own destination status. In the mid-1990s, 85% of the passengers through Narita were in-transit to another destination.

While the airline is now losing much of that US-China/SE-Asia transit traffic, there has been a proliferation of flights into China as the demand for non-stops to more Chinese destinations has soared.

According to Japan Airlines' and All Nippon Airways' figures, the number of non-stops between Japan and China has grown from just eight city pairs in 1990 to 45 in 2004. In 1990, only Osaka and Tokyo were connected with China, whereas today, 16 cities in Japan have flights to China.

Aircraft Technology
& Range Evolution

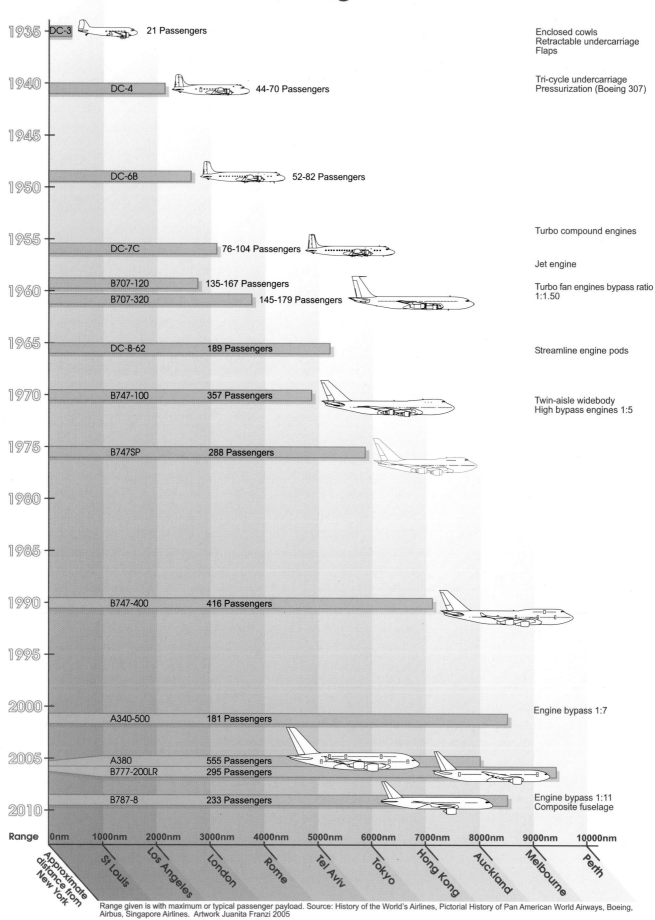

Year	Aircraft	Passengers	Technology
1935	DC-3	21 Passengers	Enclosed cowls, Retractable undercarriage, Flaps
1940	DC-4	44-70 Passengers	Tri-cycle undercarriage, Pressurization (Boeing 307)
1950	DC-6B	52-82 Passengers	
1955	DC-7C	76-104 Passengers	Turbo compound engines
1960	B707-120	135-167 Passengers	Jet engine
	B707-320	145-179 Passengers	Turbo fan engines bypass ratio 1:1.50
1965	DC-8-62	189 Passengers	Streamline engine pods
1970	B747-100	357 Passengers	Twin-aisle widebody, High bypass engines 1:5
1975	B747SP	288 Passengers	
1990	B747-400	416 Passengers	
2000	A340-500	181 Passengers	Engine bypass 1:7
2005	A380	555 Passengers	
	B777-200LR	295 Passengers	
2010	B787-8	233 Passengers	Engine bypass 1:11, Composite fuselage

Range 0nm 1000nm 2000nm 3000nm 4000nm 5000nm 6000nm 7000nm 8000nm 9000nm 10000nm

Approximate distance from New York: St Louis, Los Angeles, London, Rome, Tel Aviv, Tokyo, Hong Kong, Auckland, Melbourne, Perth

Range given is with maximum or typical passenger payload. Source: History of the World's Airlines, Pictorial History of Pan American World Airways, Boeing, Airbus, Singapore Airlines. Artwork Juanita Franzi 2005

The power of LCCs

"We focus on non-stops. It's what the customer wants and it's a lot cheaper to fly non-stop."
– Gary Kelly, CEO Southwest Airlines

There can no more emphatic endorsement of the non-stop argument than that of Kelly's, when he was interviewed by leading trade journal *Air Transport World's (ATW)* Editor in Chief Perry Flint in April 2005.

Texas-based Southwest Airlines created the blueprint for the Low Cost Carrier (LCC) revolution that has transformed air travel over the past 20 years. In April 2005, the airline had 417 Boeing 737s operating 2,900 flights a day to 59 destinations in 31 states and has been profitable in 31 of the last 32 years. The success of Southwest Airlines and other LCCs such as JetBlue (which uses the Airbus A320) has seen the LCC share of the US domestic market climb from 7% in 1990 to 25% in 2004, according to the European Low Fare Airline Association (ELFAA) report *Benefits of Low Fare Airlines 2004*.

David Neeleman's JetBlue Airways is another great LCC success story.

JetBlue took to the air on February 11, 2000 with the inauguration of services between New York's John F Kennedy International Airport and Fort Lauderdale, Florida. In early 2005, the airline served 30 cities around the US and Caribbean with 68 Airbus A320s. The airline had orders and options on a further 233 A320s, plus orders and options for 200 Embraer 190s to open more non-stops to smaller regional airports.

While JetBlue is based in New York, it flies to many secondary airports. An excellent example is the Los Angeles area, where the airline operates a host of daily non-stops to secondary airports like Long Beach, Ontario and Burbank rather than serving Los Angeles International Airport (LAX). The airline has virtually no hub operation. Reinforcing the popularity of non-stops on JetBlue's website, in May 2005, the airline touted five new non-stop services to start during that month.

Countering the success of these and other LCCs, US giants, such as Delta Airlines and Northwest Airlines, added non-stops in 2005 to lure passengers. According to the *New York Times* (Micheline Maynard, May 4, 2005), in the 12 months to May 2005, Delta had added 44 non-stop flights, Northwest Airlines had added 39, while American had put on 10 new direct routes – with more to come later in 2005. Continental (16) and US Airways (25) had also joined the trend.

In Europe, the message is the same with LCC giant Ryanair and its fleet of Boeing 737s. Founder and CEO Michael O'Leary told *ATW* in April 2004 that Ryanair was "strictly a point-to-point operator and shivered at the thought of a hub operation." The airline has 12 bases and the key to the airline's runaway success is its strategy of flying to uncongested low-cost airports. In 2005, Ryanair expects to carry over 34 million passengers on 220 routes across 19 European countries using over 100 new Boeing 737-800 aircraft. The airline has another 125 on firm order for delivery up to 2012.

According to the ELFAA report, "the low cost model is dependent on direct point-to-point flights, no transfers and short-haul flights." The report cites the European Commission (EC), which reported in 2004 that there had been a 30% increase in new routes in Europe since 1993.

Twin-engine Northwest Airlines A330s and American Airlines 777-200ERs are regular visitors to Tokyo's Narita Airport operating non-stop from US cities. *Geoffrey Thomas*

The marketing power of the non-stop

Ever since the advent of the 747 in 1970, the market has assumed that long-haul passengers would rather fly on a twin-aisle airplane than a single-aisle aircraft – even if that meant a change of plane at a hub.

Continental Airlines has debunked that notion with its new single-aisle narrow-body 757 services to Europe from Newark, New Jersey. The airline serves 13 trans-Atlantic markets with its 757 fleet from Newark, including nine cities in the United Kingdom and Ireland. The operation is so popular that Continental is adding winglets to its 757s to add an extra 300nm range to access more markets in Europe – all non-stop.

The domination of non-stops across the Atlantic is extraordinary. To London (Heathrow and Gatwick) alone, there are 650 weekly flights to and from 21 US cities. From Chicago, there are non-stop flights to 13 European cities, whereas in 1984 there was just one flight – to London.

Since the twin-engine 250-seat Boeing 767 launched ETOPS flights across the Atlantic in

February 1985, there has been a proliferation of non-stop services. In 1984, all trans-Atlantic flights were made by three and four-engine jets. Today, those types account for just 4% of flights.

Across the north and central Pacific, the situation is similar with twin-engine 777, 767 and A330 flights opening up new non-stops and outnumbering the 747 and MD-11 types, according to OAG figures.

Not so long ago, Tokyo's Narita International Airport was dubbed "747 city" but since the easing of ETOPS requirements to 207-minutes in the late 1990s, the airport is now home to United, Delta and American 777-200ERs and Northwest A330s. Northwest Airlines has recently introduced A330-200s in a 243-seat configuration on services from the US to Tokyo.

According to OAG figures in August 2004, the 747's share of departures at Narita had plummeted from nearly 80% to just 40% in seven years. This drop in share was accelerated by the opening of an additional runway freeing up landing and departure slot constraints.

In Hong Kong, the story is similar. The 747s had a 45% share when

Hong Kong's airport was based at Kai Tak with its single runway and its spectacular but difficult approach. Since the opening of Hong Kong International Airport with its parallel runways, the 747's dominance has waned and now accounts for only 18% of departures.

With the demand for non-stops, movements at airports are dominated by smaller aircraft – not 747 types. An excellent example is Heathrow where 350-450 seat aircraft only make up 90 of the 630 daily departures.

Another illustration of this is the world's busiest airport, Atlanta's Hartsville Airport in Georgia, which accounted for 85 million passengers in 2004. Virtually all (98%) aircraft movements are by aircraft with between 50 and 300-seats and Delta Airlines – which dominates the airport – has as its largest aircraft the 285-seat 767-400ER.

The domination of smaller aircraft at Atlanta's Hartsville Airport underscores data from the OAG, which shows that globally over the past 20 years:

- Non-stops have leapt from 5,700 to 10,400
- Frequencies have almost tripled
- Average size of aircraft has declined slightly

Giants for slot-limited airports

On December 24 of any year, most airlines would just love a 2,000-passenger aircraft to move all the travelers who want to get home for the holiday season. Problem is that it would be useless for the other 364 days of the year.

But for airlines that are restricted in the number of slots they can obtain into airports such as Heathrow and LAX, an aircraft larger than the 747-400 makes sense. Some airlines such as Emirates, Qantas and Singapore Airlines are "slot-limited" into Heathrow, an airport important to their marketing strategies, and they were among the first to order the 555-seat Airbus A380.

Certainly, Boeing believes that the market for the A380 will not be as great as Airbus hopes but one thing is certain, the market could never justify the investment by Airbus and Boeing in two competing 500 to 600-seat jumbos. The last such battle –

between Lockheed and MDC in the 1970s – saw both manufacturers crippled and eventually exiting the commercial market.

Boeing believes that the market size for aircraft of the 747 size and above is 790 units through 2023. Boeing suggests that 400 will be 400 to 500-seat aircraft and the balance will have more than 500-seats. Airbus holds the view that sales of its 555-seat A380 will be 1,262 in the same period.

Airbus argues strongly that Asia/Pacific population concentrations mean that long-haul flights to the region will not become fragmented like trans-Atlantic operations, and therefore, airlines will need greater numbers of bigger aircraft. And while it is true that there are a number of heavy population concentrations, such as Singapore and Hong Kong, it is also true, argues Boeing, that there are many population centres in North America and Europe that want non-stop flights to Asia. So the market will fragment at one end only.

Boeing also points out that, unlike many US and European airports, the major hubs in Asia have extremely modern airports with plenty of runway capacity to handle more flights – and they have aggressive governments that want to attract more services.

In Japan, there is another twist to the debate. Japan Airlines (JAL) and All Nippon Airways (ANA) have used all-economy 747s with up to 563 seats for domestic flights. However, with the advent of the more economical 777-300 with 525 seats in a similar configuration and an additional runway at Narita (and a fourth planned at Haneda Airport), both airlines are phasing out some of their domestic 747s. Japan Airlines said that "with a 40% increase in take-off and landing slots at Haneda (from 2008), JAL will improve customer convenience, enhance operational efficiency through a better match of supply to demand and expand its network with the 787."

The A380 cavorts about the sky at the 2005 Paris Air Show.
Mark Wagner / aviation-images.com

Singapore Airlines launched the world's longest non-stop flights in 2004 from Los Angeles to Singapore and from New York to Singapore with Airbus A340-500s. *Airbus*

Future evolution

Passengers' demands are relentless. More frills but lower fares, more comfortable seats but lower fares and more convenient schedules but lower fares.

To meet the ever increasing requirements, airlines are striving to become more flexible. Australia's Qantas has launched a low-fare international airline, a domestic LCC and an international LCC – all to meet the varied demands. Others, such as Aer Lingus and Air New Zealand, have reinvented themselves to respond to a demanding and unforgiving market.

According to Taneja, one key is to "optimize the fleet structure for flexibility and customer value". He argues that "to prosper in the new customer-driven marketplace, successful airlines will adapt new fleet strategies that balance their customers' needs with the economic necessity of managing airline capacity and demand. In this environment, fleet planning at conventional airlines will be driven by the need for greater flexibility."

He adds that "passengers are fed up with conventional airlines which fail to deliver value. Price sensitive passengers feel that they are paying for services they do not really value. Passengers paying premium fares feel that they are

not receiving value commensurate with the high fares they pay. Since many business passengers do not themselves pay for their travel, what really counts is a schedule – high frequency, non-stop services – that saves time, as long as travel guidelines of their companies are respected."

A major key to helping airlines meet varying passenger demands is an aircraft type that can perform as many missions as economically possible. The 787 promises to be the most flexible aircraft Boeing has ever built with a wide range capability and two different model sizes at launch – a first for Boeing or Douglas. The 787 will be equally at home on the Tokyo-Osaka route with a high density layout for 400 and in a 223-seat configuration for Singapore-Helsinki.

Airbus also lends support to the point-to-point theory. In its *2004-2023 Global Market Forecast*, it states that "opportunities will continue to emerge for profitable new routes to develop with aircraft like the A330 and A340 [and 777, 787 and A350]. These new long-haul routes are largely centered on the trans-Pacific, with

some of the more developed Europe to Asia markets."

Two of the world's longest non-stop air routes, Singapore to Los Angeles and Singapore to New York, have been pioneered by Singapore Airlines using the Airbus A340-500. The development also coincided with the availability of aircraft with better range and economics, which offer airlines new market opportunities. Indeed, in the past 10 years, the A340 alone has opened up 32 new routes on the Europe-Asia flow. Over the next ten years, Airbus forecasts that up to 60 long-haul routes could be opened profitably on the trans-Pacific market and between Europe and Asia.

One airline that uses both the hub-to-hub, hub-to-point and point-to-point strategies extremely well is Korean Air. The airline has targeted China's growth and the huge US market by connecting 15 Chinese cities, through its brand new Inchon International Airport hub, with 14 cities in the US. The airline is using a combination of 747-400s, 777-200/300s and A330s to link these cities and has also ordered both the A380 and 787.

chapter5
Genesis of the Dream Machine

Any sufficiently advanced technology is indistinguishable from magic.
– Arthur C. Clarke –

Boeing's 757-200 (pictured) like its larger brother, the 767-400, was being squeezed out of the market. Something radical was needed.
John Dibbs via British Airways

The birth of Project 20XX

What moment defines the true birth of a new jetliner program? Depending on who you ask, the answer could be anywhere between the first firm order and the moment in the middle of the night when a product development engineer sits bolt upright in bed shouting "Eureka!" as he scribbles a sketch of "the perfect aircraft".

Try as you might, there are no such easy answers for the 787, which emerged from a process that, on the face of it, had more in common with the evolutionary theories of Charles Darwin than the basic tenets of Aerospace 101.

It could all have been so different when studies into a new airplane family began in the latter half of the 1990s. At the time, Boeing had successfully launched the 777 into service and was selling the newly-developed Next Generation 737 like hot cakes. Design work on new variants of the 747 also continued under the 747X initiative, but it was not the super-large or smaller markets which beckoned Boeing. Instead, the real focus was on an emerging new opportunity in the middle of the market.

Casting a glance into the crystal ball, it did not take rocket science to see the next product development study had to be in the 180 to 300-seat range. Covering this range for Boeing were the stalwart duo, the 757 and 767.

These trusty twin-jets, introduced as stablemates at the start of the 1980s, had proved phenomenally successful. Between them, they had effectively proved the viability of big, high-tech twins for everything from long-range, over-water (ETOPS) flights, to transcontinental hub-and-spoke operations in the domestic US.

But times were changing, and the pair was besieged on all sides. From within, Boeing's own 737 development – particularly the stretched -800 – was nibbling cannibalistically at the US market, the true home of the 757 powerbase. A stretched 757-300 model, though wonderfully economic, did not help much. The -300 was the victim of bad timing, emerging at the low point of one of the worst downturns in US airline history.

From without, the 767 was under attack from Airbus, the acknowledged inventor of the wide-body twin, and now selling the popular A330-200. With longer legs than the 767-300ER, the newer Airbus was proving a threat to Boeing, which knew it would take more than the recently-developed 767-400ER to stem the tide.

The January 2001 announcement that Boeing was studying new directions under an initiative dubbed "Project 20XX", therefore, came as little surprise when it was formally revealed by then Chairman and Chief Executive, Phil Condit. "We're going to look at where the market is" was his bold statement at the 2000 annual results press conference. Few could have foretold the roller-coaster ride that was about to begin.

The sleek lines of the Sonic Cruiser captured the imagination of the aviation world. *Boeing*

Sonic surprise

In January 2001, news began to leak out that Boeing's newly unveiled "Project 20XX" included a sensational surprise. Although no drawing had been seen outside Boeing, rumors were rife of a distinctive aircraft with a sharply-swept, delta wing shape similar to Concorde but with a sharp break outwards in the sweep angle about halfway along the leading edge – the likes of which had never before been seen.

Sure enough, on March 29, 2001, Boeing revealed the truth to an astonished aerospace world. It was indeed looking at an "unconventional configuration" 767-size design with aft-mounted engines and a range of 8,000nm or more. But it was speed, rather than size or range, that grabbed the world's attention.

The sleekly shaped jet was designed to cover these vast intercontinental distances at cruise speeds between Mach 0.95 and 0.98. This would save three hours over a 747 on a route such as Singapore-London, two hours on a polar New York-Tokyo journey and as many as five hours over a conventional one-stop London-Sydney service. The concept bordered tantalizingly close to the supersonic range without actually crossing over into the phenomenally expensive development that marked the financial doom of the Anglo-French Concorde project over 30 years earlier.

Developed in strict secrecy, the high-speed aircraft was equipped with canards – small wing-like control surfaces that regulate the up and down or pitch motions of the aircraft. The concept aircraft had been given the mysterious codename "Project Glacier". Now, with airline enthusiasm growing, Boeing Commercial Airplanes President and Chief Executive Officer, Alan Mulally, renamed the daring concept the "Sonic Cruiser" in deference to its transonic operating speed.

The aircraft was aimed at cruise speeds 15 to 20% faster than current airliners but with operating costs similar to the 767-300. Boeing saw this as the ultimate expression of its long-held belief in the fundamental shift away from popular trunk routes to a more "fragmented" route structure connecting city pairs that, in some cases, had never before seen international services.

But was the Sonic Cruiser the ultimate "fragmentor" of Boeing's dreams? There was only one way to find out, and that was to get the airlines involved – just as it had with the 777 program a decade before. In late May 2001, it therefore invited representatives of a dozen key airlines to help further define the Sonic Cruiser.

There was no shortage of volunteers. Boeing was flooded with calls from airlines wanting to know more. It seemed Boeing had hit the jackpot…or had it?

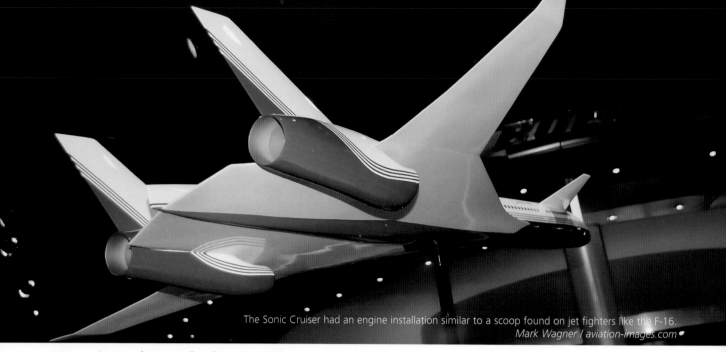

The Sonic Cruiser had an engine installation similar to a scoop found on jet fighters like the F-16.
Mark Wagner / aviation-images.com

Engine breakthrough

Engine technology, an important design driver in any new aircraft concept, was even more crucial in the Sonic Cruiser. From the outset, Boeing based its early design work on the highly capable, very advanced, high-thrust engines originally developed for the 777.

The idea was warmly embraced by the engine makers and Boeing alike, all of them eager to make the most of existing technology that had cost billions of dollars to develop.

Then came bad news. Further wind tunnel work, computational fluid design tests, performance and emissions analyses through 2001 confirmed that unchanged 777 engines, or even significant derivatives, would not allow the design to cruise at its "sweet spot" Mach 0.95-0.98.

The problem was the size of the core, which was too small.

Speaking to *Flight International*, Sonic Cruiser Program Marketing Vice President John Roundhill said the test results "argue for a major change, if not a brand new engine."

The size of an airliner's engine core is traditionally optimized for the thrust it will need at the end (or top) of the climb after take-off. In the thin atmosphere at levels above 30,000ft, the thrust required to sustain cruise is only a fraction of that used for take-off.

However, the Sonic Cruiser's higher cruise speed meant the core had to be larger. To counteract the noise and emissions of this larger core at take-off, the low-pressure spool, or the part of the engine that compresses the air before passing it into the high-pressure core and through the combustor, would necessarily have to be larger.

Herein lay one of the main design problems. For the entire Sonic Cruiser concept to work, the design incorporated natural area ruling or shaping to prevent unacceptable drag building up at high speed. Boeing had cleverly

achieved this by mounting the engines fully aft.

To achieve the low-drag design for transonic cruise, the engines were semi-recessed or partially buried in the wing itself. This combination meant that if 777-style engines were used, they would need large fans and bypass ducts which were simply too big to fit in the available 9.2ft space of the aircraft's fighter-like "S-duct" inlets.

By year-end, all of the "big three" engine makers had begun studying completely new propulsion systems with General Electric first to show its hand – a study concept dubbed "Gen X".

Based on an 80% scale version of the high-pressure compressor of the massive GE90-115B (then in development for the longer-range 777 variants), the Gen X would ultimately morph into an altogether different powerplant for a very different application – the GEnx on the 787 Dreamliner.

For the moment, however, it seemed a new power race was underway.

Co-author Christine Forbes Smith gives perspective to the GE90-110B1 on the 777-200LR. *Boeing*

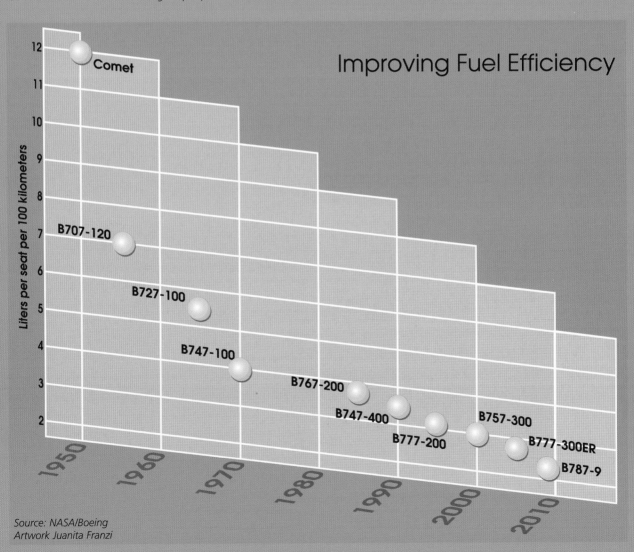

Improving Fuel Efficiency

Liters per seat per 100 kilometers

Comet
B707-120
B727-100
B747-100
B767-200
B747-400
B777-200
B757-300
B777-300ER
B787-9

Source: NASA/Boeing
Artwork Juanita Franzi

Project Yellowstone, renamed the 7E7, was unveiled in November 2002. *Boeing*

Paradigm shift - from speed to economy

The first serious cracks in the case for the launch of the Sonic Cruiser opened up at the June 2001 Paris Air Show.

The environmental lobby, openly frustrated by the US government's continued rejection of the 1997 Kyoto Protocol climate change accord, began to paint the high-speed concept as a potential bad neighbor.

These concerns assumed a much higher profile during the show when reservations were raised in an open letter from Margot Wallstrom, the European Commissioner for the Environment, to top Boeing executive Harry Stonecipher. She said: "The question is whether a one-hour time saving on a trans-Atlantic flight is worth a significant increase in CO_2 emissions contributing to climate change. In my view, the environmental price is not worth paying. Instead of building even faster planes, your industry should work towards improved environmental performance."

Boeing countered that the faster transit times, and quicker descent and climb of the Sonic Cruiser actually made it an environmentally friendly project compared to, for example, the European Concorde. Although there was no getting around the higher fuel consumption, Boeing believed that overall airline consumption would remain unchanged because of time savings generated through eliminating or reducing weather delays, direct routings and fewer take-offs and landings.

No one at Paris knew that the real threat to the Sonic Cruiser's survival would come not from lobbyists but from a devastating terrorist attack three months later in New York and Washington DC on September 11, 2001 (9/11).

It has been argued that with, or without, the debilitating blow of the attack and its aftermath on the world air transport industry, the business case for the Sonic Cruiser had already become tougher. Airlines, particularly in the US, were on course for a slump in 2001, even before the attacks, and revenues had already started to nose-dive.

The results effectively transformed the prospects for the fabulous-looking Sonic Cruiser from a premium revenue-earning flagship into a potentially expensive white elephant.

It was time for Boeing to reveal details of another ace up its development sleeve – "Project Yellowstone".

Project Yellowstone

Deep within Boeing's product development inner sanctum, another top secret project ran alongside Project Glacier. Following the same naming protocol, the initiative was named after another US National Park - in this case, Yellowstone.

Believed to date from the earliest years of "Project 20XX", of which both Glacier and Yellowstone were parts, the latter project was first revealed in May 2001 but had already been underway for at least four years. The basic plan involved applying many of the advanced manufacturing, design and systems technologies studied for the higher speed airliner to a conventional design.

Boeing planned to use this as a "reference" model against which airlines could grasp the true benefits of the advances as compared with a 767. This was intended to demonstrate the relative scale of the various advances, and to be used by the airlines as a yardstick to measure the value of speed in helping make the business case for the Sonic Cruiser.

By late 2001, it was described as "environmentally optimized" because the same advanced, lightweight structure, improved systems technology and higher efficiency engines had a lot to offer a conventional jetliner.

By June 2002, the market, still staggering after the impact of 9/11, was finding it difficult to put a serious value on speed. Although Boeing scratched its head wondering where it had got its sums wrong, the signals were increasingly loud and clear.

That same year, Air France and British Airways announced the imminent end of Concorde services, and at the same time, a three decade love affair with speed.

In efforts to keep interest alive in the Sonic Cruiser, Boeing even offered an alternative, more conservative mid-wing design, which eliminated the forward canard, easing concerns of jetway compatibility among some members of the Sonic Cruiser advisory group.

Admitting the company's uncertainty in July 2002, Mulally said: "We don't know the answer yet. If it turns out that we can't value the time saving, then we will see what the next development should be." Mulally added that using Sonic Cruiser technology on a conventional 757/767-sized aircraft offered a "dramatic improvement in operating efficiency." But he stopped short of announcing a fundamental shift in direction.

This ultimately came in dramatic style at the end of 2002, when Boeing offered a choice between three Sonic Cruiser concepts and what was by now dubbed a "Super Efficient" design. The writing had been on the wall for the Sonic Cruiser since October that year when, at an advisory group meeting, not one of the airlines gave a high rating to the Mach 0.98 cruise speed.

First real details of the Super Efficient, were meanwhile revealed by then Sonic Cruiser Vice President and General Manager Walt Gillette at a conference in Phoenix, Arizona in November 2002.

At first glance, the aircraft looked like a blend of 767 and 777, with raked wingtips, extensive use of composites, much higher bypass ratio engines and a host of advanced systems. "The airlines' choice is either to go 15 to 20% faster at Mach 0.96-0.98, or to fly at today's speed and altitude but burn quite a bit less fuel," he explained.

The airlines were unanimous. They voted for efficiency over speed. So, just before mid-December 2002, the company took the pivotal decision to shelve the Sonic Cruiser and focus instead on the "Super Efficient" aircraft.

"Our plan is to get this going," said Mulally at a year-end announcement. He added that the final swing away from speed was triggered by an unprecedented combination of "economic cycle and terrorist overhang." The new aircraft, he said, would offer 777-like range and speed, but at an astonishing 10% better operating cost per seat than the 767. Target "entry into service" date was set at 2008, the same as the Sonic Cruiser – a date which Mulally believed would "fit well with the economic recovery."

Time would tell – but for now, efficiency was king.

An airline's dream

In January 2003, the first major step towards the birth of the 787 Dreamliner took place when the Super Efficient airplane was renamed the 7E7.

No one was saying officially what, if anything, the "E" actually represented. However, Boeing had taken advantage of the demise of the Sonic Cruiser to highlight the cost-saving and "green" advantages of the alternative. Definition of the "E" could therefore be appropriate to the requirement, meaning anything from "efficient" and "environmental" to "eight."

But what exactly were the airlines hoping for? They were certainly getting a lot more than a basic replacement for the stalwart 767 but the bottom line was an unprecedented opportunity to dramatically cut operating costs and boost revenue while, at the same time, expanding into new market niches that would have been impossible with existing models.

Initially, two versions were proposed – a 210-seater and a 250-seater in three class layouts – with ranges of between 7,000nm and 8,000nm. The cross-section was still to be determined but hovered within a few inches between the seven abreast layout of the 767 and a narrower version of the nine to 10-abreast seating of the 777.

A key part of the battle to win the hearts and checkbooks of the airlines was to offer as much flexibility as possible while keeping major derivatives to a minimum. The two variants therefore quickly morphed into the 228-seat -300X and a stretched -400X seating 268. Now aimed squarely at beating the A330-200, Boeing predicted the 7E7 would enjoy a spectacular 20-25% better fuel burn per passenger than the A330 and up to 20% better than the 777-200.

By the end of March 2003, several big events took place. The first, and virtually unnoticed milestone, was Boeing's submission to the European and US authorities for both type and production certification of the 7E7. The other was the re-designation of the 7E7 and 7E7STR (stretch) and the subsequent splitting of the family into two main variants and two range categories: the baseline and stretch 7E7SR (short-range) and the baseline and stretch 7E7LR (long-range).

The split reflected the broadening scope of interest among more than 40 airlines now helping Boeing define the 7E7. Yet, as the market focus sharpened, it became obvious the split required more fine-tuning. The baseline LR was defined with 200-220 seats with a 7,780-8,000nm range and a stretched LR seated up to 260 with a range of around 7,180-7,400nm.

The baseline SR seated between 320 and 340 (in two classes), with a 3,000-3,400nm range, and the stretched SR was configured with seats for between 280 and 310 with a range of up to 4,000nm. The baseline aircraft was expected to be around 190ft long while the stretch was some 30ft longer.

The 7E7's sleek shape and shark fin tail grabbed headlines around the globe.
Boeing

Dream becomes a reality

But how could Boeing maintain as much commonality as possible and yet achieve the massive range differences, which varied from trans-continental to ultra-long range inter-continental?

The question was critical. If it could not meet the aggressive operating efficiencies promised at the start of the program, the Dreamliner would remain just that – a dream.

At least part of the answer was two different wingspans – a shorter span for the short-range pair and a larger span for the longer-range variants. Boeing's plan was to use the same basic wing structure for both pairs but with an outboard replaceable section for the short-range models, which was sketched out with a 164ft span. The longer range wings were configured with a 188ft span.

Further changes came by mid-2003, however, with the decision to simplify the model mix even further. Under the revised plan, Boeing decided to launch a baseline model and a short-range stablemate first, followed by a stretch. It decided to abandon plans for a shorter or medium-range stretch, concentrating instead on what was obviously

the key market need for the baseline model.

Overall length was by now defined around 182ft with the stretch at around 202ft. Maximum take-off weight for the baseline was in the 400,000-410,000lb range, while the stretch was to have a much higher range of take-off weight options, ranging from 480,000 to 500,000lb.

To reduce the weight penalty for the 7E7 operators interested in using the aircraft on shorter ranges, the design target range of the baseline was cut from 7,200-8,000nm to around 6,580nm, while span was cut from 190ft to 125ft.

But the changes caused some heartache among potential operators. Shorter-range users said the 7E7, as then defined, was not much better than the 767, while those looking at the baseline design wanted the range to go back up again. Combined with indecision over the growing engine thrust range (see Chapter 7), Boeing then took the key decision to redesign the short-range model with a significantly lower take-off weight and a shorter span and structurally lighter wings tailored for the domestic market.

The new wing option released the designers from the dangers of an over-compromised design and allowed the range of the baseline

to grow back up towards 7,800nm while giving the short-range optimum performance over shorter routes up to 3,500nm with a single-class layout of 300 passengers. The wingspan of the basic and stretch versions was restored to almost 194ft, with the short-range version expected to be cut back to around 170.5ft with winglets or some other lift-enhancing wingtip treatment.

By April 2004, with the engine situation clarified and potential customers happy with the specifications, Boeing revealed the finalized 7E7 line-up. The baseline aircraft, now dubbed the 7E7-8 was to carry 217 passengers in a three-class arrangement on flights up to 8,500nm. The shorter-range 7E7-3, was configured with seating for 289 in two classes for flights up to 3,500nm, while the long-range 7E7-9 was designed to carry 257 passengers in three classes with a range of 8,300nm.

With the design now refined, Boeing announced the authority to offer airlines the 7E7 on December 16, 2003.

By 2005, further "tweaks" saw the aircraft, by now dubbed the 787, revised upwards in capacity with the -8 seating 223 passengers and the -3 seating 296 passengers. The stretched -9 grew to some 259 passengers but was destined for more stretching as subsequent definition progressed.

While the 787's shape caused a stir, the concept interior created a sensation. Airline executives gushed with praise for its innovation in bringing back the magic of flying. *Boeing*

Passenger dreams - flying magic

More than any previous Boeing jetliner, the 787 was designed from the inside out. Right from the start, Boeing wanted to bring back the "magic" of flight and improve the whole flying experience.

Boeing Passenger Satisfaction and Revenue Director, Klaus Brauer, outlined the essential goals of the 787 concept. "Flying is special but we, as an industry, have almost succeeded in killing it off in a lot of people," he said. "But scratch the surface a bit and our research says people will get back to the magic of it." The 787 interiors work began from where the Sonic Cruiser had left off and was aimed at solving the problem of "what was dreadful about the passenger experience."

The basic idea of the 787 cabin was to remind passengers they were actually "flying" rather than isolate them from the experience. "It is about 180 degrees different from the other approach," Brauer said. "Everyone dreams about flying – no one dreams about things like toothpaste. They want to be flying in an aircraft not a hotel lobby."

The experience was designed to begin from the minute the passenger stepped off the jetway into the fuselage. "We can't change the small dark tunnel feeling of the jetway, so we have to 'go big'

with the cross-aisle," Brauer said. "The usual, low cabin ceiling structure is therefore replaced with a lofted back-lit ceiling, or 'sky dome'."

To emphasize the perception of a lighter, more open cabin design, the fuselage was also configured with extra-tall windows, which were recessed into overlarge sidewall embrasures. These allowed even the 95 percentile male in a center aisle seat to view the horizon above the surrounding seatbacks (see Chapter 14).

Being able to see the outside world, and particularly the horizon, was one of the main results from preliminary design studies conducted in association with interior specialists and psychologists. "We feel strongly the need to connect people with flying, and part of that is to view the horizon," Brauer said.

Other key initiatives included the use of sculpted composite arches to divide the cabin into well-proportioned zones, overhead bins deeply recessed into the sidewalls and innovative "mood" lighting designed to help the body's circadian rhythm, or internal body clock, adjust better to shifting time zones.

The 787 interior was, in all respects, just as well thought out as the exterior and formed a vital element of the hallmark design.

chapter 6

Material
Breakthrough

Dreams are today's answers to tomorrow's questions.

The "air show favorite" B-2 stealth bomber makes extensive use of composites. *Boeing*

What are composites?

Perhaps the most contentious and widely misunderstood aspect of the 787's design is the extensive use of composite materials in the fuselage and wing structures. Such comments as "the plastic airplane" and "the aircraft baked in an oven" have surfaced in the media, fueling public confusion.

What many people fail to appreciate is the long history of composite utilization in the aerospace field dating back to the 1960s and the Cold War. Although composites were extremely expensive, the demand for superior performance in the Cold War era demanded their use.

Many years of research, experimentation and refinement have produced a material that for virtually all applications is superior to the traditional aluminum structure in a number of fundamental ways. In fact, such well-known military aircraft as the air show favorite, the AV-8B Harrier "Jump Jet", and the awesome show-stopper, the B-2 stealth bomber, have made widespread use of composites in load-bearing structures (see graphic on page 53).

Composites are lighter, stronger, do not corrode, have excellent resistance to high temperatures and much lower maintenance requirements than aluminum. But what exactly are composites and how are they used?

The term composite simply refers to a material made from two or more different ingredients which, when combined, takes on the properties of each and provides benefits beyond those of the individual constituents. Such materials have been used in a variety of applications for decades.

Commonplace items, such as golf club shafts made from graphite composites, hockey sticks made from thermoplastic composites and Kevlar bullet-proof vests, all have unique properties of being lightweight, flexible and strong due to the distinctive combination of materials used.

In the case of the 787, the particular composite used in more than 50% of its airframe by weight will be Carbon Fiber Reinforced Polymer (CFRP). In simple terms, it is a polymer (or resin) acting as the bonding agent which is combined (or reinforced) with strong woven carbon fibers.

Fine carbon fibers are entwined together into larger bundles known as yarns. These yarns are then interlaced into a loose mat or ribbon where the fibers are either randomly oriented or aligned into a unidirectional tape (depending on the types of load the material will experience).

The resulting tape is then wound around a mold and saturated with polymer to form what is known as a "prepreg". This prepreg is put under pressure with the use of hot gases in an autoclave to ensure the polymer completely infiltrates the reinforcing fibers. Once cured, the result is an extremely strong and lightweight material.

A composite structure can also be made with a liquid molding where the manufacturer mixes the carbon-fiber and resin in various ways to produce the end product.

The myths exposed

The slow introduction of composites into commercial airplane production on a wide scale is not the result of doubts about its viability, as some have suggested. It is actually the outcome of having to invent completely new, efficient and economically viable large-scale production methods.

Composites have been used for many years in smaller but vital airplane structures, such as the 777 tail and horizontal stabilizer and floor beams, which were relatively easy and economical to manufacture. In contrast, the composite wing on the AV-8B and virtually the entire B-2 bomber were laid up by hand – costing billions.

The durability of the composites has been outstanding. The 787 Chief Project Engineer Tom Cogan explained: "Now that [the 777s] are reaching a point in their life where the airlines are opening them up for duty inspections, they are finding the composite parts in perfect order." Vice President for the 787 Mike Bair concurred, saying: "One of the things we did was look at in-service experience and maintenance history on the 777 horizontal and vertical tail and we found there's never been maintenance action in-service on that structure."

Bair also pointed out that Boeing had been using composite

material on its aircraft dating back to rudders for the 737 and DC-10 in the 1970s, which showed no signs of wear when the aircraft were retired recently.

Aluminum and other metals will continue to have a role in certain structures on airplanes. For most of the larger sections of the fuselage and wing, as well as the moving wing flaps, and in areas prone to corrosion, CFRP composites have hugely beneficial qualities. Reductions in the number of parts required (due to their construction as single pieces) and the resultant weight savings are just the start.

Around 25% of the Airbus A380 is composed of composites in such areas as the vertical and horizontal tail, tail cone, flap track fairings, centre wing box, wing ribs and undercarriage gear doors, indicating a general acceptance of composite utilization in some important components of the largest commercial airplane built. In fact, Airbus declares that its use of composites on the A380 center wing box alone, a structure which binds the wings to the fuselage, will reduce weight by 1.5 tons. Airbus has also gone for an all-composite wing on its A350 competitor for the 787.

The big jet engine manufacturers, such as Pratt & Whitney, Rolls-Royce and General Electric (GE), have also used composites extensively for many years in such engine components as fan blades. Their use of these materials is constantly expanding, although the types of composites used differ somewhat from those employed in airframes due to the

requirement for the engines' highly specialized parts to work efficiently in conditions of extremely high temperatures.

According to Melbourne-based Hawker de Havilland's (HdH) GM Business Development Tony Carolan, one of the best examples of the successful use of composites is in Formula One racing cars. "They used to be built just like aircraft and the racing teams used to hire aerospace engineers to help design the cars," he said. "But in the 1990s, they turned to composites because they were stronger, lighter and resisted fire."

Australia's HdH, now a Boeing subsidiary, is a Tier One (T1) Supplier on the 787 program for all the 787's trailing edge control surfaces and is also a supplier to Airbus of a variety of control surfaces and parts for the A330 and A340 and of the wingtip for the A380.

Carolan added another dimension to composites' resistance to fire. "We have recently had a composite tail cone certified for the Bombardier Challenger executive jet because of the risk of fire from the Auxiliary Power Unit [APU]," he said. "This is normally made of titanium or stainless steel."

Durability of composites is extraordinary, Carolan said. "We have replaced the wing flaps on the C-130J Hercules transport for air forces. The earlier metal flaps normally start cracking after 3,000 hours. We stopped testing the composite flaps at 60,000 hours!"

To the surprise of no one at Boeing, the first full-scale fuselage section was completed in December 2004 demonstrating the production processes to be employed in 2006. The 22ft long one-piece structure has no rivets or seams. *Boeing*

Weaving a miracle

In December 2004, Boeing completed the first full-scale fuselage section made from composite material as a graphic demonstration of the manufacturing methods that will be employed for the 787 production process in 2006.

The huge, one-piece structure was 22ft long and about 19ft wide – the first of eight pieces from different sections of the airplane that will be built through 2005. The unveiling of the rivet-less, seamless structure was undoubtedly a proud moment for those involved in the development of the 787 – final proof that the building of huge single-piece sections of fuselage could be done.

Surprisingly, the inspiration behind the process came from a sail-making company, North Sails Group, which had developed a method of applying lightweight composite ribbon via multiple heads, all working on the same mandrel, to make a mainsail or jib. Boeing licensed the technology and set about up-

scaling the size of the operation. It constructed a mandrel or mold, shaped as a mirror image of the inside of an airplane fuselage piece, around which the composite tape would be wound. It was then wrapped and placed in a giant autoclave (the largest ever constructed) for curing for several hours at 250°F.

When completed, the piece was unwrapped, inspected and removed from the rotating tool with the help of a massive Swedish forklift called the Max Move. The next steps were cutting out the windows and doors and testing the application of paint, as well as exhaustive testing to verify its structural integrity.

Walt Gillette, Vice President 787 Airplane Development, had a wry smile during the unveiling when he said: "This is a piece of aviation history. Nothing like this is in production. We are now seeing how all advanced airplanes will be built from this time forward."

Composite Materials

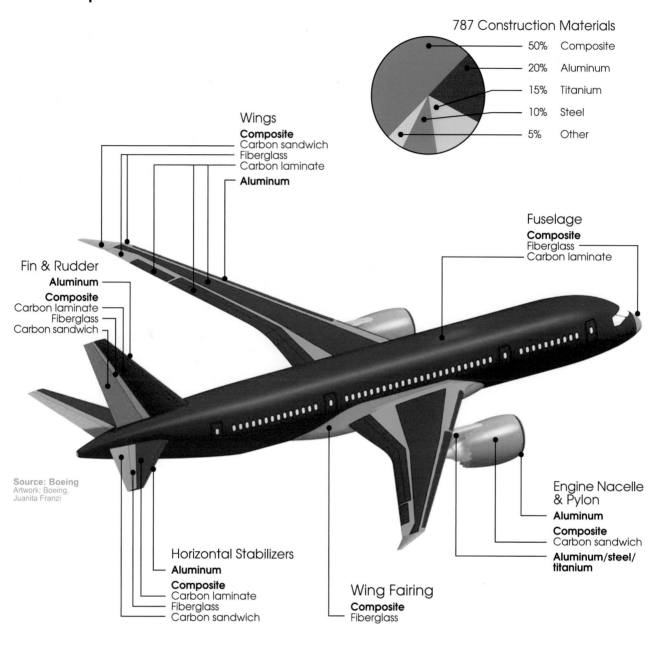

787 Construction Materials

- 50% Composite
- 20% Aluminum
- 15% Titanium
- 10% Steel
- 5% Other

Wings
Composite
Carbon sandwich
Fiberglass
Carbon laminate
Aluminum

Fin & Rudder
Aluminum
Composite
Carbon laminate
Fiberglass
Carbon sandwich

Fuselage
Composite
Fiberglass
Carbon laminate

Engine Nacelle & Pylon
Aluminum
Composite
Carbon sandwich
Aluminum/steel/titanium

Horizontal Stabilizers
Aluminum
Composite
Carbon laminate
Fiberglass
Carbon sandwich

Wing Fairing
Composite
Fiberglass

Source: Boeing
Artwork: Boeing,
Juanita Franzi

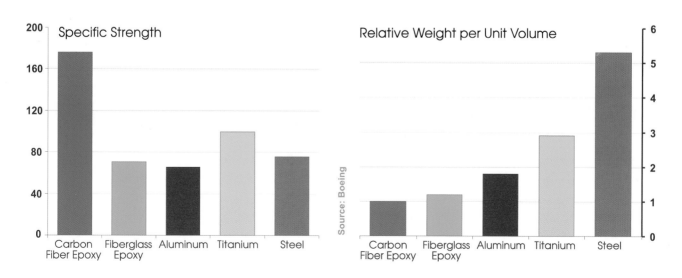

Specific Strength

200
160
120
80
40
0

Carbon Fiber Epoxy · Fiberglass Epoxy · Aluminum · Titanium · Steel

Relative Weight per Unit Volume

6
5
4
3
2
1
0

Carbon Fiber Epoxy · Fiberglass Epoxy · Aluminum · Titanium · Steel

Source: Boeing

Stronger than steel

Traditionally, the biggest degree of wear and tear on an airplane's structure comes from constant pressurization/depressurization cycles through a lifetime of take-offs and landings.

To achieve cabin pressurization, the airframe must be inflated like a balloon. Current aluminum fuselages are built to withstand a pressure equivalent of 8,000ft altitude, the lower pressurization altitude of 6,000ft requiring a much stronger and heavier fuselage. The composite fuselage on the 787, which is significantly stronger and lighter, is designed to withstand a pressurization level of just 6,000ft.

In addition, the added strength of the composite fuselage enables the size of windows to be enlarged significantly. Both of these factors ensure a much more comfortable flying experience for passengers, an aspect that will be discussed in more detail in Chapter 14.

To demonstrate the strength of composites and to convince airline executives of its strength, the Boeing sales team developed a unique hands-on exercise. Each member of an airline evaluation team was invited to attack a 3ft by 4ft piece of composite skin and a similar piece of aluminum with a hammer.

Almost immediately, the aluminum piece showed significant distortions and dents, whereas the composite piece remained intact even after continual pummeling. The conclusions were obvious.

The issue of "ramp-rash" (see Chapter 12) – or damage caused to the aircraft on the ground from service vehicles while loading and unloading – is also addressed by the use of composites. "Such incidents cost airlines some $2 billion each year in damages," Bair said. A big maintenance burden, and consequently a financial burden, is significantly reduced with the use of composites.

As Cogan explained: "We have a design criterion that's called Barely Visible Impact Damage so that, if from 5ft away you cannot see damage, then there is no need for repair." Even when the damage is visible in composites, a temporary repair kit is in development, which will allow a temporary repair to be completed in as little as an hour. This will enable the aircraft to fly to its home base for a more permanent fix.

With aluminum airplanes, however, loading incidents require immediate repair as small cracks in a piece of metal can spread rapidly. This adds significant costs for the airline as a result of rescheduling or canceling of flights, not to mention the cost of the repair itself.

Corrosion busters

Corrosion is a critical issue for airplanes manufactured from aluminum and is the major focus of complex maintenance inspection schedules for airlines flying these airplanes.

Moisture has a cumulative and insidious effect on aluminum and metal structures over time. In aircraft, moisture accumulation and condensation, as it drips down the inner surface of the fuselage and around the lavatories and galley, brings about significant corrosion in vulnerable and often hard-to-access areas.

It also adds to the maintenance burden airlines must factor into their running costs to replace the parts adversely affected by moisture incursion over time. To help minimize this, the pressurized air inside the cabin is kept at a sufficiently low level of humidity to prevent the effects this moisture will inevitably have on the airframe. This dryness, in turn, affects the comfort levels experienced by passengers.

As the composites used on the 787 do not corrode, the level of humidity in the pressurized cabin air can be increased from around 5% to 15%, creating a more comfortable environment for passengers.

Consequently, the factor of corrosiveness will no longer be an issue requiring regular inspection by maintenance engineers on the 787. This level of durability will allow line maintenance intervals

The lightness and strength of composites was a key factor in its application on the wing for the AV-8B Harrier, built by McDonnell Douglas, now part of Boeing. *Boeing*

to be pushed out to 1,000hr compared with 500hr for the 767 or 700hr for the A330. In fact, heavy structural maintenance checks, known as D-checks, which are generally performed after six years, can now wait for 12 years.

One of the keys to more efficient aircraft is weight reduction – and the concomitant benefits of reduced airport landing charges, lower fuel burn, higher load capacity and longer range. By using composites, the 787 will push the weight/efficiency envelope well beyond any other aircraft currently flying. In fact, the "787 will lick the envelope", one engineer said.

On the manufacturing side, the benefits of composite fuselage sections are undeniable. On traditional aircraft, one metal barrel requires around 1,500

sheets of aluminum held together by nearly 50,000 rivets. With composites, the number of fasteners and rivets drops by 80%. Together with fewer support structures in the strong one-piece sections on composite aircraft, the weight savings are significant.

The lessons of parts savings have come from work in military programs, both in the US and Europe, where part counts have plummeted. The US Joint Strike Fighter program requires half the parts and just 10% of the tooling of the F-18, one of the aircraft it is designed to replace.

The 787's airframe is expected to be 20% lighter than those made from aluminum which, together with other factors, will translate to 20% fuel savings and 10% lower seat mile costs.

GE introduced composite blades in 1995 on its GE90 which powered British Airways' first 777s. *John Dibbs via British Airways*

Composite blades

Composites are also at the cutting edge of aeroengine development. General Electric Company (GE) has already initiated tests for its new GEnx engine that advances the use of composites in jet engines in ways never before experienced.

The GEnx is the only jet engine being developed with the front fan case and fan blades made of composite materials – a breakthrough that will provide greater engine durability and dramatic weight reduction, the company claims.

At GE Transportation's headquarters in Evendale, Ohio, the company ran a successful but brutal "blade-off" rig test using a composite fan case and composite blades. In the test, a fan blade is released while the engine operates at full speed. The composite fan case maintained its structural integrity while containing the released blade. The force of the blade release is the equivalent of a staggering 100 tonnes.

In an understatement, Tom Brisken, General Manager of the GEnx program, said: "Simply put, the concept of a composite fan system worked, and worked well." The first full GEnx engine will go to test in 2006, with engine certification scheduled for 2007.

Carbon fiber and epoxy resin composite materials are a key to GEnx performance. The composite fan case will reduce engine weight by 350lb, or 700lb on the 787. Overall weight reduction is more than 800lb for the aircraft because composite materials also save weight in the engine installation. The weight reduction translates directly into fuel burn savings, which either increase payload or range.

GE introduced the first composite fan blades in jet travel in 1995 with the GE90 engine on the Boeing 777. During nine years in airline service, the GE90 composite fan blade has proven to be extraordinarily reliable, with no special inspections or repairs ever required.

The most recent GE90 derivative, the GE90-115B/110B1 for the 777-300ER and 777-200LR, introduced composite blades that were designed using three-dimensional aero-technology. GEnx composite fan blades will be produced using the same fibers, resin and manufacturing processes as the GE90 fan blade.

The GEnx fiber-braided composite fan case, to be the first in commercial service, results from more than 20 years of GE research and development, including testing on a NASA demonstrator engine. In addition to weight savings, the fan case's composite properties create a tough, hard structure that eliminates the potential for corrosion.

chapter 7
Engines to Soar

Every major advance in aviation has been linked to the aircraft engine.
– Donald Douglas Jnr –

Pratt's promise

Pratt and Whitney (P&W) maintained a veil of secrecy over its proposed engine for the 787 until October 2003, when it revealed the first details of a design dubbed the PW-EXX.

P&W was able to claim its proposal as the only all-new engine offering for the 787, the competition having already thrown in its lot with derivative designs based on their respective 777 engines (see pages 59 and 61).

Along with its competitors, P&W faced the huge challenge of designing an engine that would not only satisfy Boeing's demands for a 15% fuel burn improvement over the 767-300ER but one that would work as efficiently over short hops as it would over ultra-long-range inter-continental routes.

P&W PW-EXX Program Director at the time, Peter Smith, commented: "We're looking at whatever we have to do to meet the 'book ends' around both 8,000nm and 500nm, which is a huge range to meet with one engine. We are all looking at innovative ideas to solve this equation."

The two-spool, counter-rotating design incorporated a direct-drive, 112in diameter fan made up of 24 "dual arc" wide-chord, hollow titanium fan blades. The counter-rotating spools were a significant technical advance which increased the efficiency of the engine by matching the spinning turbine blades with the direction of the gas flowing through the core of the engine. These were based on the fan design used in the Engine Alliance GP7200 engine, then in its early development stages with General Electric, for the Airbus A380.

The 10-stage high-pressure (HP) compressor was based on the advanced F119 military engine used on the latest USAF frontline fighter – the F/A-22 Raptor. The F119 was also the first large military engine in which P&W had counter-rotated the low-pressure (LP) and HP spools.

To meet the more-electric needs of the 787, the PW-EXX was also configured with a core-mounted gearbox located on the inner part of the engine rather than on the nacelle or cowling, as well as dual 225KvA starter generators. To be environmentally friendly, it was also designed with the latest Talon X low-emissions combustor and low-smoke producing fuel injectors taken from military powerplants, such as the F-35 Joint Strike Fighter engine.

To make its bid more competitive, P&W planned to shorten the detailed design phase while lengthening the test phase by 10 months. Compared to the long 56-month PW4000 test effort on the 777, for example, it aimed to go from engine launch to certification in just 36 months. This would mean bringing forward key test work on the flying test bed by a whopping 21 months compared with the 777 effort.

The vital fan-blade containment test would be conducted some 18 months earlier. This is probably the most dramatic (and expensive) test in the certification of an engine. It involves detonating a small explosive charge at the base of a fan blade while the engine is running at full power. The debris is sucked through the engine, which must then be capable of a controlled shutdown without becoming violently destabilized due to the imbalancing loss of a blade. To pass the test, the engine must totally contain all parts of the debris which impact the inside of the nacelle with explosive velocity.

There was no doubting the conviction of P&W, which knew the 787 was a "must-win" contest to keep alive its role as a leading player in the big jet game. As P&W Commercial Engines President Bob Leduc said to *Flight International* in February 2003: "We do believe Boeing is going to do the program and we are going to be there. It's that simple, and come hell or high water, we are going to win."

GE - engine powerhouse

General Electric (GE), the world's dominant engine maker, was equally determined to get a piece of the action on the Dreamliner. It established its civil jet empire with the CF6 – a highly successful powerplant derived directly from the TF39 military engine, which it had developed in the 1960s for the Lockheed C-5A Galaxy. It had spent much of the 1990s considering a modern successor in the 40-70,000lb thrust class.

The TF39 was the world's first "big fan" or high bypass ratio engine. Unlike earlier generation turbojets, or early turbofans, the TF39 had a dramatically larger fan at the front of the engine. This, in turn, drove a large volume of air through an annular duct that "by-passed" the core. The by-passed air not only added a lot of thrust at take-off but also wrapped around the jet blast from the core and smothered it like a muffler, reducing noise and improving efficiency.

Although it had continued to grow the CF6 and add several improvements, it had eagerly leapt on the 787 as the perfect target for a next-generation successor. GE immediately began studies based on a scale of the much larger GE90 core. As a baseline, it aimed for a 15% fuel burn reduction versus the CF6-80 models powering the 767 and

A330. It also looked at a pressure ratio close to 50 for the new engine, compared with up to 42 for the GE90 on the 777.

The initial concept was based on a 60-70% scale of the GE90 core but built in a mass of high-tech improvements from an initiative effort called Gen-X (Generation-X), which was aimed at "seeding" the ground for a new generation of engines. Target bypass ratio was around 11:1, but no more.

Judging the bypass ratio was a tricky balancing act. As the engine makers approached higher and higher bypass ratios, the noise went down but the drag of the wider engines began to rise dramatically. Judging the "sweet spot" in the delicate trade-off between the two was pivotal to the final overall performance of the aircraft in terms of range, payload, speed and noise.

For noise, Boeing had set a goal of meeting London Heathrow's QC1 noise limit for departure and QC0.5 for approach which, all the engine makers agreed, was far tougher than Chapter 4 noise standards.

The Chapter levels define maximum allowable EPNL (Effective Perceived Noise Level) in relation to aircraft maximum take-off weight and are measured at sideline, fly-over and on approach as set by International Civil Aviation Organization (ICAO). Chapter 4 is the strictest and applies to all aircraft introduced after January 1 2006.

However, Quota Count (QC) noise limits were introduced by airports

in England to reduce noise at night. Aircraft are given QC ratings based on noise made on take-off, fly-over and landing. It governs the number of arrivals/departures allowed throughout night-time operations. The noisier the aircraft the higher its QC rating and the fewer allowable movements. Quietest aircraft have a QC rating of 0.5. The QC1 limit of 92.9dB or less will apply to the 787.

By mid-2003, it emerged that the GEnx would also include, not only a composite fan derived from the pioneering design of the GE90 but also a composite fan case. It would have an integral vane frame and a low single annular TAPS (twin-annular pre-swirl) combustor (a specially developed form of high-tech burner that mixed fuel and air in a more thorough fashion), thereby reducing the amount of emissions to the atmosphere. The concept had a new low-pressure turbine design with fewer blades and stators, which offered big maintenance savings downstream. Stators are fixed vanes that help guide the flow of gas or air through the engine.

Other features included a de-coupling device that separated the fan from the shaft in the event of a serious blade-failure and prevented the engine passing on dangerous loads to the airframe.

With the recent success of achieving GE90 exclusivity on the longer-range 777s, GE felt increasingly confident about its 787 bid.

Development of Power and Fuel Efficiency of the Jet Engine

Thrust (Thrust-lbs)
SFC (Specific Fuel Consumption)

Source: Rolls-Royce
Artwork Juanita Franzi

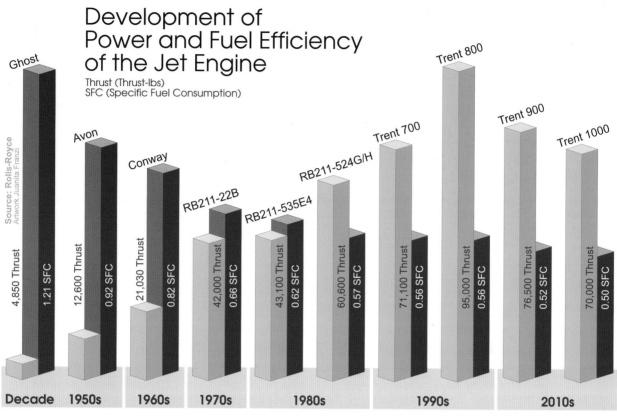

	Ghost	Avon	Conway	RB211-22B	RB211-535E4	RB211-524G/H	Trent 700	Trent 800	Trent 900	Trent 1000
Thrust	4,850	12,600	21,030	42,000	43,100	60,600	71,100	95,000	76,500	70,000
SFC	1.21	0.92	0.82	0.66	0.62	0.57	0.56	0.56	0.52	0.50

Decade	1950s	1960s	1970s	1980s	1990s	2010s

Frank Halford (de Havilland Engines), Sir Frank Whittle (inventor of the jet engine), Sir Geoffrey de Havilland and C. C. Walker (de Havilland Aircraft) pose with prototype Comet in 1949. *BAe Systems*

Rolls-Royce - Trent heritage

Since entering the big fan club in the early 1970s with the RB211, Rolls-Royce had become fiercely competitive with a family of newly developed versions named after the River Trent, which flows through central England.

Unlike either of its US competitors which used two-shaft designs, Rolls-Royce had adopted a three-shaft concept for its larger thrust powerplants. This meant that, in addition to the standard low and high-pressure spools, the Rolls engine also incorporated an "intermediate" (IP) spool.

The UK engine maker believed this allowed the three separate compressors (LP, IP and HP) to run much closer to their optimum speeds, making it inherently more efficient. As the overlapping shafts in the engine could physically compress more air in a relatively shorter space, the Rolls engines were also distinctly shorter than their US counterparts. The engine maker said this made the design stiffer and less prone to "shaft whipping" or bowing, therefore helping with performance retention over the lifetime of the engine. As with cars, performance in aircraft engines declines over time.

The Trent line traced its ancestry to a series of engine concepts developed in the 1960s (see graph opposite), which culminated in the RB211 developed for the Lockheed L-1011 TriStar. Despite its promise, the engine could not have had a worse start to life. Development difficulties with the engine's innovative composite fan, made from a carbon-fiber material called "Hyfil", delayed the program so much that it forced Rolls-Royce into bankruptcy in 1971 – seriously threatening the TriStar program. The company was rescued by the British government, and development and eventual entry-into-service of the RB211 continued successfully with a conventional titanium fan.

From this difficult start, Rolls-Royce mounted an amazing comeback with a series of highly reliable and powerful engines, including the RB211-535E4 for the 757, which featured the world's first wide-chord fan blades. This refers to blades that are far wider in width (or chord) than the previous generation of narrow-blade designs. Building on this and the RB211-524, which was used on the 747 and later TriStar models, Rolls-Royce began a dramatic expansion in the 1990s with the launch of the Trent family of derivatives. This began with the 67,500-72,000lb thrust Trent 700, which entered service on the Airbus A330 in 1995, and the Trent 800, providing thrust up to 95,000lb for the 777, which entered service in 1996.

These laid the foundations for the later Trent 500, which was used on the A340-500/600 in 2002, and the Trent 900, which was scheduled to power the first commercial services of the A380 from early 2007. It was from this much stronger competitive position, therefore, that Rolls-Royce entered the battle for the 787 with a concept provisionally dubbed the RB262.

The design was based largely on the architecture of the Trent 900 with increased bypass ratio. Outlining the architecture in 2003, Rolls-Royce Director Engineering and Technology Mike Howse said the "more-electric" and "no-bleed" requirements of the 787 matched the three-shaft concept particularly well. It incorporated technology from the company's "Vision 10" initiative, and the European-funded ANTLE low-emissions engine demonstrator. ANTLE is a European research and technology program which stands for Affordable Near-Term Low Emissions.

In particular, it gave Rolls-Royce the chance to counter-rotate the IP spool, rather than the HP spool and use the intermediate shaft, rather than the usual LP spool, to extract electrical power. The design also included a smaller spinner which allowed more air to pass through the engine without having to increase the fan diameter.

In advance of the upcoming engine competition, Rolls-Royce also dubbed the design the "Trent 7E7", stopping short of a formal designation until it was sure of success.

Rolls-Royce's Trent 1000 is based on the Trent family of engines, such as the Trent 800 (pictured here). *Rolls-Royce*

Battle for the Dreamliner

With the hard-won experience of the 747 and 777 programs behind it, Boeing decided almost immediately that there was no way that three engine types would be offered on the 787.

The cost and time of certifying three engine-airframe combinations on both the 747 and 777 programs had proven an enormous strain and Boeing believed the benefits of a three-way choice to the market simply could not be justified for the 787. This view was also, to a lesser extent, shared by the engine makers themselves who agreed it was better to compete for all or half the market, rather than attempt to claw back billions of dollars worth of investment against two other challengers.

Furthermore, the surprise 1999 decision to offer engine exclusivity to GE for the 777-200LR/300ER caused speculation that Boeing may be tempted to follow suit for the 787. Vice President 787 Program, Mike Bair, kept everything hanging in the air when he confirmed in mid-2003 that "we will select one or two (engine suppliers), and which one or two, later this year."

However, engine makers took some comfort from the fact that the market prospects for the 787 made it a completely different business case compared with both the longer-range 777 and the competing A340-500/600 program. For this, Airbus too had opted for the sole engine supplier route with the selection of the Rolls-Royce Trent 500 in 1997.

In both cases, the market potential was much smaller than that for the 787 sector, which was conservatively estimated at around 3,000 over 20 years, and the hugely varied customer base virtually demanded the competitive pressure of an engine choice.

Battle lines between the "big three" were effectively drawn in mid-February 2003, when the engine makers were officially given targets for take-off, climb and cruise performance, as well as fuel consumption, emissions, environmental noise and installed weight. The briefing also spelled out the overall fuel consumption/seat target which was set at around 17% better than the 767-300ER, while the operating cost target against the same aircraft was firmly pegged at 10%. Gross weight was also to be lighter than the A330-200.

From the outset, GE pursued the idea of exclusivity, having become sole supplier for the longer-range 777s and, with French engine maker Snecma in the CFM International joint venture on the CFM56, for the highly successful 737 family. Rolls-Royce and P&W, meanwhile, began under the assumption that half a share was better than no share at all.

What is "no bleed"?

Boeing was determined the 787 would be the most efficient airliner ever built and, although structural, aerodynamic and systems improvements would address almost two-thirds of this, a major part of the benefit would come from the new engines.

To help engine makers achieve this paradigm shift in efficiency, Boeing decided that nothing less than a fundamental rethink of the power generation needs of the aircraft would do. The result was a shift to a more-electric aircraft concept (see page 71) that relied heavily on electrical power generation for many of its systems needs, rather than the more conventional high-pressure air or pneumatic system.

Traditionally, aircraft systems such as the cabin pressurization, de-icing and environmental control systems were powered using hot high-pressure air taken or "bled" from the high-pressure compressor of the engine. Boeing argued that if these systems were powered electrically then there would be no need for bleed air. It followed that the mass flow of the engine, and the overall efficiency of the engine, would increase if the need for bleed was eliminated.

The argument goes beyond pure theoretical physics. Without bleed, there was no requirement for the pneumatic system and no complex array of piping, ducts, pumps, control valves, brackets and heat exchangers that usually made up the bleed air ensemble. As most of the ducts were normally made of heat-resistant but heavy titanium, this saved a huge amount of weight.

Just as importantly, the elimination of the complex bleed and pneumatic systems cut out a significant amount of monitoring and maintenance. It was also, Boeing argued, a safety enhancement as it kept super-heated air in the engine, where it belonged, instead of spread through the plumbing of the wing root where the heat exchangers are normally located.

All this was possible because of advances in power electronics technology, much of which had been studied for the Sonic Cruiser. It was also just as importantly, a result of both Boeing and the engine makers "thinking outside the box", when it came to the search for never-before-seen levels of efficiency in an air transport aircraft.

General Electric's GEnx is based on the successful GE90 seen here undergoing demanding water ingestion tests. *General Electric*

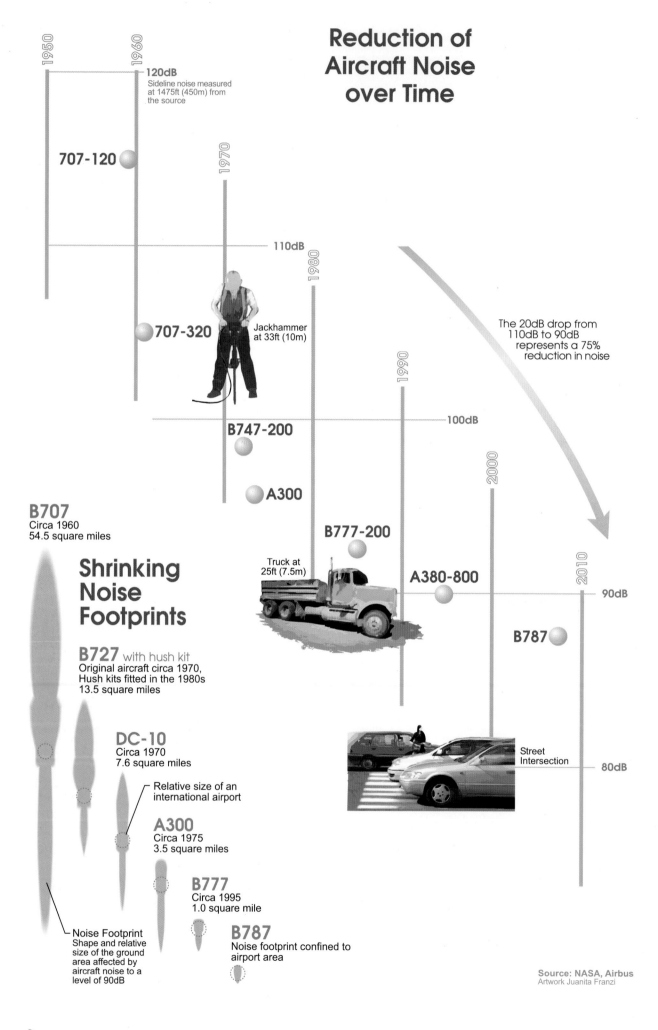

Reduction of Aircraft Noise over Time

1950

1960

120dB
Sideline noise measured at 1475ft (450m) from the source

707-120

1970

110dB

1980

707-320

Jackhammer at 33ft (10m)

The 20dB drop from 110dB to 90dB represents a 75% reduction in noise

1990

B747-200

100dB

A300

2000

B777-200

Truck at 25ft (7.5m)

A380-800

2010

90dB

B787

Street Intersection

80dB

Shrinking Noise Footprints

B707
Circa 1960
54.5 square miles

B727 with hush kit
Original aircraft circa 1970, Hush kits fitted in the 1980s
13.5 square miles

DC-10
Circa 1970
7.6 square miles

Relative size of an international airport

A300
Circa 1975
3.5 square miles

B777
Circa 1995
1.0 square mile

Noise Footprint
Shape and relative size of the ground area affected by aircraft noise to a level of 90dB

B787
Noise footprint confined to airport area

Source: NASA, Airbus
Artwork Juanita Franzi

Going green

While "efficient" was considered the original definition for the "E" in 7E7, many believed "environmental" was just as applicable. This was not only because the engines were designed to be the quietest, most efficient, and "greenest" ever developed in terms of emissions but also because they were part of an integrated new design.

As Walt Gillette, Vice President 787 Airplane Development, explained: "It is the integrated effect that allows our improvement to be so dramatic. You can only take full advantage of these technologies with a brand-new airplane." For example, if the engine is more efficient, the fuel requirement drops. If less fuel is needed, the wing can be smaller and, therefore, the overall aircraft can weigh less. If the aircraft weighs less, the required engine thrust is lower and this, in turn, reduces fuel demand. "This allows another cycle of downsizing everything – the wing, the engines and so on," Gillette said.

The overall changes gave Boeing confidence that the 787 would use 20% less fuel than any other aircraft of its size, of which just over a third would result directly from advanced engine technology. By early 2005, with the aircraft more clearly defined, Boeing was able to put this in more specific terms.

On an internationally agreed basis of liters of fuel consumed per 100 passenger-kilometers, and assuming a full aircraft on a 3,000nm sector, Boeing estimated the 223-seater 787-8 would come in at around 2.6 liters versus 2.9 liters for the 301-seater 777-200ER and 3.2 liters for the A340-300E or 3.8 liters for the 280-seater A340-500. The 787-9 fared even better, with an estimated fuel burn of 2.4 liters per 100 passenger-kilometers, or roughly similar to a large family car – with the obvious exception that this "car" traveled at close to the speed of sound!

For noise, Boeing set the aggressive target of 24 EPNdB (environmentally perceived noise decibels) below the internationally agreed Stage 3 noise levels in force by the early 2000s.

In terms of pollutants, it also pushed the engine makers to develop combustor technology that would achieve nitrous oxide (NOx) production 36% below the levels set by the ICAO Committee on Aviation Environmental Protection (CAEP) Level 4. GE, for example, set a goal of less than 4 liters/1,000kg (1 US gallon/450lb) of NOx at an overall engine pressure ratio of around 47:1.

Even the airframe was designed to make less noise and was becoming more of a focus for aerodynamicists and noise engineers as engines became quieter. Simpler flaps, wing leading edge high-lift devices, chevron shapes on nacelle trailing edges (see page 68) and less cluttered landing gear shapes, all helped to guarantee the 787 would indeed become the first true "green machine" of the 21st century.

The quiet, smokeless 787 engines will be in stark contrast to the early turbojets of 1959 on this American Airlines Boeing 707.
Charlie Atterbury

Engine exchange

Boeing came up with other innovations to make the 787 attractive to both operators and lessors.

For the first time on any commercial jetliner, it designed in the ability for the aircraft to be re-equipped with an alternative manufacturer's engines within a target of 24 hours (see page 99).

The unprecedented initiative, revealed in March 2004, just before the final engine supplier choice was announced, took the industry by surprise. It was, however, a logical extension of the "more-electric aircraft" philosophy, in which the aircraft systems were less directly dependent on being plumbed into the power plant, and which could therefore be "unplugged" with relative ease.

So what was all the fuss about? Why was it so hard to change engines and why did that affect aircraft values? Historically, the evolution of airframe-engine combinations had always been closely intertwined and, even in later generations, the cost of modifying an airframe to take a different engine often had been prohibitive.

This was a big deal to leasing companies in particular, as in the past, the choice of engines could have a limiting effect on the residual value of the aircraft. For example, an airline might want to take an aircraft but only if it was able to use one powered by a specific engine manufacturer. If the lessor could offer the airframe and the ability to interchange engine types to suit the operator, the value of the aircraft would remain higher for longer.

Bair said the idea gave "the airlines a lot of downstream flexibility and will increase the finance ability of the aircraft if you can have more than a single engine offering." The idea of a modular engine swap-out capability had originally been adopted for the Lockheed Martin F-35 Joint Strike Fighter to enable seamless interchangeability between the competing F135 and F136 engines.

"The idea is that the hook-up will be identical at the wing," Bair said. Operators, he said, would be able to "un-bolt and rehang the replacement, and there will be a software roll in the flight deck for the different engine. One of the reasons we can do this is the capability of today's avionics. We can make it all-software programmable."

Cross-section of the GEnx engine for the 787
General Electric

Rolls-Royce's successful Trent family of jet engines was a major advantage for the British company's bid to get aboard the 787. *Rolls-Royce*

Changing course

Boeing originally planned to make its engine selection by the end of 2003 but as the year drew on, it became increasingly clear that the thrust requirements for the short-range 787 and its longer-range siblings, were becoming too divergent.

The company had been constantly fine-tuning the three proposed variants – the short-range (787SR), the baseline model and the stretch version – as they strove to meet airline demands. To make the SR more attractive, the airlines told Boeing they needed significantly lower operating costs.

The result was a drastic revision of the design. "To make sure it's going to be a spectacular short-range aircraft, we're going to be making the wing lighter by de-gauging it," Bair said. The wheels, brakes and fittings were also lighter, along with other changes such as winglets at the end of a smaller 165ft wing span.

The change left the engine makers scrambling to figure out how to cover a much wider thrust range which, ideally, now dipped well below 50,000lb for the 787SR, and well above 70,000lb for the stretch.

Inevitably, Boeing decided it had to delay its engine selection until well into 2004. Bair said the engine makers were "getting a bit nervous with the timing in front of us." The slip gave the engine makers more time to study the options, including "one engine more specialized for the SR marketplace, or maybe one for the SR and base and another for the stretch," he added.

Sure enough, in early January 2004, Boeing issued what was expected to be the final requirements document for the engines, with proposals for two distinct engines covering the 55,000-60,000lb thrust range for the short-range/baseline 787, and a 70,000lb-plus thrust class version for the stretch. Within Boeing and among the engine makers, the proposal was dubbed the "one-and-a-half" engine study, because of the frustratingly close thrust requirements.

The complication was more than frustrating – it was counter-intuitive to the entire "simpler is better" approach of the 787. It was with great relief to all concerned that Boeing returned to a common engine in late February. "The logic to stay with our original plan is overwhelming," Gillette said. "When we began, we had one engine build across the fleet and that's been our mainstay. We spent six to eight weeks looking at 'what if' we had a sort of engine-and-a-half family with a common core and two fan sizes. In the end, we saw that the value and simplicity of one engine build is somewhat better."

The shift came because "when we looked at the short-range (or 787-300SRX as the SR was dubbed), we saw it needed plenty of climb power, and the more we looked at the stretch (by then known as -400X), the more we saw it was a really efficient aircraft that needed slightly less power than we thought," Gillette said.

The stage was set for the long-awaited final engine decision, now due in April 2004.

The winners emerge

On 6 April, 2004 Boeing announced that General Electric and Rolls-Royce had been selected to power the 787 while Pratt & Whitney, the only manufacturer proposing an all-new design, had been rejected.

Bair said the final selection had been "a very close decision, but we are happy this represents the best value for everyone who is going to be involved in this aircraft." He added that "technically, all three had very robust offerings that met or exceeded our requirements." The final decision had been based on a "combination of all aspects" including technical, marketing and financial aspects.

The GE engine, subtly re-designated the GEnx, and the newly named Rolls-Royce Trent 1000 were to be certificated at 70,000lb thrust for the heavier 787 models, with a de-rate to 53,000lb for the short-range version. Under a brand-new Boeing nomenclature, this variant was now called the 787-3, while the 8,500nm range baseline was the 787-8 and the stretch, the 787-9.

Both engines were targeted at first run in 2006, although the identity of which engine would lead the program with first flight and certification would obviously depend on which was ordered first by the launch customer.

GE's engine, a fifth generation GE90 derivative, was by now defined with an 111in diameter high-flow swept composite fan, incorporating "fewer" blades than the 22-blade set used on the 777. In fact, to the industry's surprise, GE would ultimately reduce the final blade count to only 18. The Trent 1000, meanwhile, officially became the fifth member of the Trent family and featured an 112in diameter, highly swept fan rooted in a smaller hub.

David Calhoun, President and Chief Executive Officer of GE Transportation, said of the win: "Needless to say, this is one of the biggest days in the history of our jet engine business." Mike Terrett, President of Civil Aerospace at Rolls-Royce, said: "This is a special day in the long and successful relationship between our companies. Now, once again, our focus is on bringing a new generation of Trent successfully to market."

P&W President Louis Chenevert conceded that, while his company was disappointed, "we thank the entire PW-EXX team for their outstanding efforts in this hard-fought competition." Although he stressed that advanced technologies developed for the PW-EXX would be used to "pursue other opportunities in the commercial engine market," the 787 loss confirmed P&W's gradual relegation to third place in the big engine league. Inevitably, more of the emphasis for its future commercial work would be placed on its International Aero Engines (IAE) partnership and sister company P&W Canada.

chapter8
Beneath
the Skin

Imagination is more important than knowledge.
Albert Einstein

Into the future

If the advanced composites, engines and more-electric systems were the bones and muscles of the 787, then the Common Core System (CCS) was the central nervous system of the new jetliner.

Awarded to Smiths Aerospace of the UK in February 2004, the CCS made the most of advances in rugged, powerful computing technology to form a single platform that would take the place of up to 100 different line replaceable units (LRUs), or black boxes, dotted around a conventional airliner. By concentrating all the processing functions of many different systems in one area, the design saved a significant amount of weight as well as offered increased performance, lower costs (both in acquisition and maintenance), and took less time to update.

The concept, or at least the first real working example of anything like the CCS on a Boeing airliner, had been tried on a smaller scale in the 777 with a valuable device called the Aircraft Information Management System (AIMS). The AIMS collected, formatted and distributed onboard avionic information for the bulk of the aircraft's major systems, including flight management, engine thrust control, data communications management, flight data recorders and the operation of the flight deck displays. It even kept careful watch over the aircraft's health through condition monitoring.

Now, with the CCS, Smiths would take this even further, tackling more systems and connecting the higher processing "brains" of the main CCS (which, like AIMS, was made up of two dual redundant Common Computing Resources cabinets), with mini-brains housed throughout the aircraft known as Remote Data Concentrators. To keep the various systems separated within the main processing brain of the CCS, the system was designed around an ARINC 653 "partitioned software operating environment" – a series of artificial barriers that isolated the various software sets.

The data would also whiz around the system at far higher speeds using an avionics full duplex switched Ethernet (AFDX). Also known as an ARINC 664 Deterministic Ethernet, it connected the CCS with the Remote Data Concentrators, avionics and utility systems at speeds up to 1,000 times faster than the predecessor ARINC 429 used in earlier generations of airliners.

The decision to use Ethernet-based technology also meant the system could benefit from the massive amount of commercial investment that had been poured into it since its invention in 1972, compared with the more arcane and aviation-specific data communication systems such as ARINC 429 or the military standard MIL-STD-1553 databus. It was also inherently more flexible and therefore capable of growing with the 787 and its future systems development.

They say "beauty is only skin deep" but on the 787, the real beauty is the Common Core System well below the flashy exterior. *Boeing*

Electrifying experience

Boeing took a deliberate step into the 21st century when it decided the 787 should be its first "more electric aircraft". But what did this actually mean?

The basic concept was to use electrical power in place of pneumatic or, in some cases, hydraulic power wherever possible. The approach had been the study of research and development work for decades but, like the Ethernet electronics technology discussed earlier, it was not considered sufficiently mature or low-risk until recently. Limited more-electric technology had been applied on the F-35 Joint Strike Fighter and the Airbus A380 but the 787 was by far the most extensive "electric jet" yet designed.

As with every other aspect of the 787 design, the aim was to reduce costs of ownership and operation as well as improve performance, increase flexibility, simplify maintenance and enhance passenger comfort. The more-electric concept helped achieve each of these goals by lowering the number of parts, allowing key subsystems to be more closely integrated and enabling fewer parts to perform more tasks. This saves weight, reduces fuel burn and increases aircraft performance.

The electric jet also cruises more efficiently because the engine is used more appropriately for thrust, and power is extracted from the low or intermediate pressure spool (see Chapter 7), rather than the high pressure spool.

Design flexibility is also improved because with a more-electric aircraft there are fewer high temperature ducts and flammable liquids involved, eliminating many of the design features required to handle the remote possibility of in-flight fires, such as automatic hydraulic fire shut-off and fire protection. Lighter materials such as aluminum and composites can also be used in place of titanium and other heavier fire-resistant materials.

More-electric proponents say reliability is improved because electric systems are easier to monitor and diagnose, and the integration of power generation provides more back-up capability and functional availability. Hamilton Sundstrand was selected to supply the bulk of the electrical generation, distribution and electrically-reliant systems on the aircraft in early 2004 when it was awarded the first of several contracts covering the electrical power generation and start system, environmental control system, remote power distribution units and auxiliary power unit (APU). It later also picked up the contract to develop six power panels that controlled and distributed electrical power on the 787.

Electricity is generated by two 250 kVA generators attached to each of the two engines plus two additional 225 kVA generators connected to the APU. Converted and "conditioned" from variable frequency power, the energy is used to de-ice the wings through an electrothermally-operated, rather than a pneumatically-powered, system. Electrical power is also used to actuate the undercarriage, control the brakes, drive the environmental control and cooling systems, and even start the engines – a major task, which traditionally used high pressure bleed air from the APU.

Pilots rated on the 777 will feel right at home in the 787 cockpit (shown). *Boeing*

On display

The 787's futuristic flight deck display system befitted a 21st century flagship aircraft yet was still designed to enable pilots to transition easily to and from other members of the Boeing family.

Using the specially-developed STAR (shortened transition and rating) conversion training course, Boeing developed the 787 flight deck to be so familiar to 777-rated pilots that it would take only five days "differences" training for crews to transition from one to another.

Similarly, the transition time for 757/767 crews already covered by a common type rating, was eight days to the 787. It was also eight days for 737-600/700/800 and 900 pilots to the 787, while 747-400 transition training was a more extensive 10 days.

Continuing the "glass cockpit" evolution that had begun at the start of the 1980s with the relatively limited displays on the 757 and 767, and which had really taken off with the A320, 747-400 and 777, the 787 flight deck has more display area than any previous Boeing jetliner – but fewer actual screens than the 777. The display on the 787 was dominated by five 9in by 12in (15in diagonal) Rockwell Collins flight displays, four in a row across the cockpit panel and one on the center pedestal forward of the throttles.

"We're talking about double the display area, and liquid crystal displays (LCDs) that push the state-of-the-art," said 787 Program Assistant Chief Pilot Mark Feuerstein, who added that "the 777-rated pilot will feel right at home in a 787." Pilots of the larger Boeing twin-jet would be familiar with the display format as well as other instruments, including the Thales-supplied integrated standby flight display LCD, also found on the 777. This presented pitch and roll attitude, airspeed, altitude, heading and landing approach deviation data in a mini-version of the primary flight displays.

"The wheel, column and rudder pedals are also common to the 777," Feuerstein said. "The controller has to have a large displacement so each pilot can see and understand what the other pilot is doing to control the aircraft. They are always linked and the throttles are back-driven, so the crew can always understand what the autopilot is doing. All three elements are important for situational awareness."

Rockwell Collins also supplied the display control panels, multifunction keypads and cursor control devices that could be used, even in severe turbulence, to operate some functions via the screens in a "point and click" fashion. The new features were expected to go beyond the positive piloting experience developed by Boeing for the 777.

"It's my assertion that, from the pilot's view, the 777 is the easiest, most predictable and satisfying civil airliner ever designed," Feuerstein declared. "It's our job to replicate that on the 787."

Advanced avionics

The 787 was designed to navigate with pinpoint precision to any place on the planet using a Honeywell-supplied suite of sophisticated avionics dubbed the "Nav" package.

To ensure absolute accuracy and multiple redundancy, the Nav suite included both the tried-and-tested inertial reference system (IRS), as well as the latest version of the more recently developed satellite-based navigation (Satnav) system. The IRS was descended from the original inertial navigation systems developed in the 1960s for US nuclear submarines and the Apollo space program, and has been improved upon ever since.

By measuring acceleration, the IRS provided a primary reference for long-range navigation and for attitude control, indicated true heading, pitch and roll, cross-track deviation, track angle error, miles to waypoints and drift. An associated air data system, measuring aircraft speed and altitude, was also part of the package, in addition to two micro-IRS units, which were available as back-ups. Two attitude heading reference systems, based on the off-the-shelf units supplied to regional airliners, were also included for further back-up.

The Satnav capability was housed in a pair of multi-mode receivers called the INRs, or integrated navigation receivers. This plugged into signals from conventional ground-based navigation systems such as the standard instrument landing system (ILS), which provides guidance to runways, and marker beacons and en-route Nav waypoints called VORs (VHF omni-directional radio).

It also picked up signals from the constellation of global positioning system (GPS) satellites in geostationary earth orbit to provide an extra layer of GPS-provided positional data, as well as the very latest in GLS (GPS landing system) capability. This would enable the 787 to make landings using the ILS in the worst Category (Cat) IIIB weather conditions, as well as the newly established Satnav-based Cat 1 GLS approaches to airports covered by differential GPS ground stations.

Other elements of the Nav package include dual distance measuring equipment (DME) transmitters, two radio altimeters and optional dual ADF radios, as well as the emergency locator transmitter (ELT), which triggers if the aircraft is forced to make an emergency landing and loses all power.

As part of the package, Honeywell was also contracted to provide the Crew Information System/Maintenance System (CIS/MS) which gives the crew a constant watch on the general health of major aircraft systems. This system built on the central maintenance computing (CMC) and airplane condition monitoring functions provided by Honeywell for the Boeing 777. The tool had proved invaluable to 777 operators in helping maintenance engineers isolate faults and troubleshoot problems.

The CIS is linked to a secure crew wireless local area network (LAN) which will be used with wireless LANs in airports to upload flight plan information, cabin manifests and passenger information. The system will be powerful enough to reach the aircraft at up to 400ft, allowing information to begin loading before the aircraft has even docked. The system will also allow maintenance engineers with wireless laptops to access maintenance data without even having to board the 787.

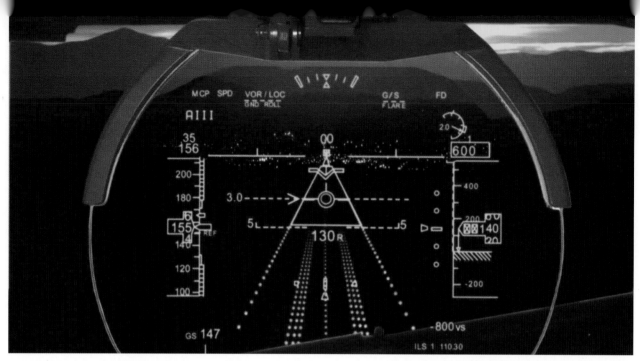

MCP SPD   VOR/LOC   G/S   FD
          GND ROLL   FLARE
AIII
35
156
200
180   3.0- - - →
155   5L   J5   140
140
130R
120
100
GS 147   -800vs
                         ILS 1 110.30

Rockwell Collins HGS, similar to the one pictured, will be standard on the 787. *BAE SYSTEMS*

Field of view

One of the most striking visual aspects of the 787 flight deck, compared to all the current Boeing wide-bodies, was the positioning of dual Rockwell Collins Flight Dynamics Head-up Guidance System (HGS) in the overhead panel directly in front of each pilot.

Originally developed for use in combat aircraft as an outgrowth of gun sight technology, the HGS has evolved into a valuable system to improve situational awareness in commercial and business aircraft. The HGS projects primary flight guidance information directly into the pilot's line of sight onto a transparent glass screen. The information is also projected with its focus at infinity, which means that a pilot can read the screen while maintaining a constant view directly ahead of the aircraft.

Unlike earlier HGS, such as those introduced on the 737 Next Generation from the turn of the 21st century onwards, the 787 HGS was based on a pin-sharp LCD image source, rather than the conventionally used cathode ray tube technology. This important step not only improved overall image quality but provided the platform for a wider range of uses later in service.

These could include a future enhanced vision system (EVS) in which the HGS projects flight guidance imagery, combined with a synthetic or augmented view of the real world outside, uses data from an array of on-board sensors such as infra-red cameras or millimeter wave radars. "Future possibilities could include EVS or three-dimensional synthetic vision, though we're not currently offering those," Feuerstein said. "But they could definitely find their way onto the flight deck in the future."

Boeing opted for the dual-HGS configuration as a standard after "the tremendous experience we have had on the 737s, which are only delivered with one system in place," Feuerstein added. "They're a major safety enhancement and provide for future growth capability."

The 787 HGSs would be the latest generation of devices from the Portland, Oregon-based Flight Dynamics stable, building on the successful HGS4000 series and finding wider applications throughout the industry, including Embraer's E190 family of "E-Jets".

Along with the HGS and flight deck head-down displays, Rockwell Collins was selected to supply a communications suite that included VHF radios, satellite communications, voice and data high-frequency radios and cockpit and flight data recorders. It was also chosen to provide a sophisticated safety and situational awareness system, comprising terrain warning, weather radar, and Traffic Collision Avoidance Systems (TCAS) (see pages 136 and 137).

787 Internal Systems Suppliers

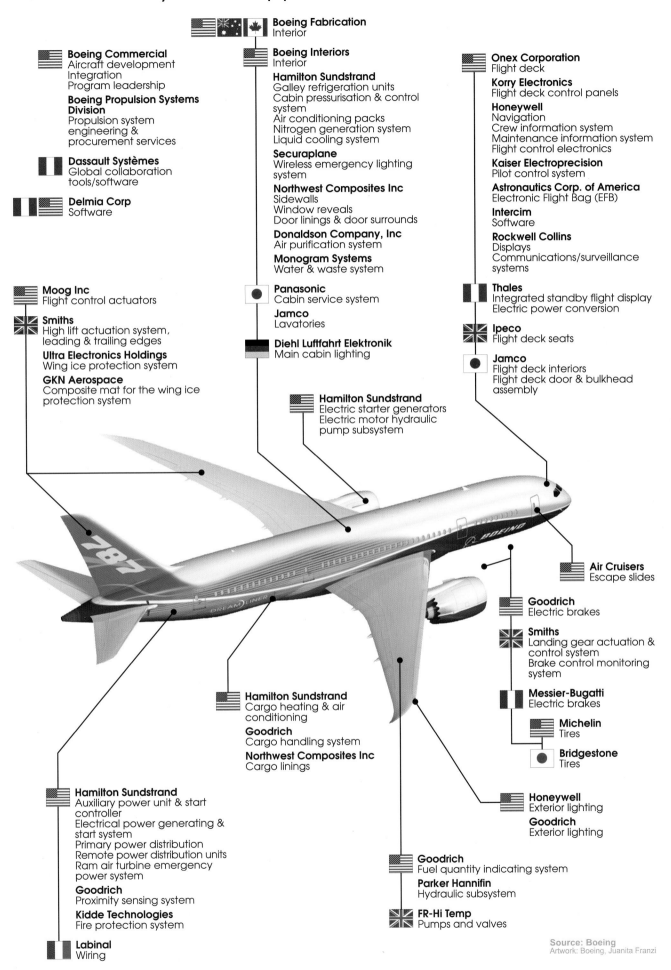

Boeing Fabrication
Interior

Boeing Commercial
Aircraft development
Integration
Program leadership

Boeing Propulsion Systems Division
Propulsion system
engineering &
procurement services

Dassault Systèmes
Global collaboration
tools/software

Delmia Corp
Software

Boeing Interiors
Interior

Hamilton Sundstrand
Galley refrigeration units
Cabin pressurisation & control
system
Air conditioning packs
Nitrogen generation system
Liquid cooling system

Securaplane
Wireless emergency lighting
system

Northwest Composites Inc
Sidewalls
Window reveals
Door linings & door surrounds

Donaldson Company, Inc
Air purification system

Monogram Systems
Water & waste system

Panasonic
Cabin service system

Jamco
Lavatories

Diehl Lufftfahrt Elektronik
Main cabin lighting

Onex Corporation
Flight deck

Korry Electronics
Flight deck control panels

Honeywell
Navigation
Crew information system
Maintenance information system
Flight control electronics

Kaiser Electroprecision
Pilot control system

Astronautics Corp. of America
Electronic Flight Bag (EFB)

Intercim
Software

Rockwell Collins
Displays
Communications/surveillance
systems

Thales
Integrated standby flight display
Electric power conversion

Ipeco
Flight deck seats

Jamco
Flight deck interiors
Flight deck door & bulkhead
assembly

Moog Inc
Flight control actuators

Smiths
High lift actuation system,
leading & trailing edges

Ultra Electronics Holdings
Wing ice protection system

GKN Aerospace
Composite mat for the wing ice
protection system

Hamilton Sundstrand
Electric starter generators
Electric motor hydraulic
pump subsystem

Air Cruisers
Escape slides

Goodrich
Electric brakes

Smiths
Landing gear actuation &
control system
Brake control monitoring
system

Messier-Bugatti
Electric brakes

Michelin
Tires

Bridgestone
Tires

Hamilton Sundstrand
Cargo heating & air
conditioning

Goodrich
Cargo handling system

Northwest Composites Inc
Cargo linings

Hamilton Sundstrand
Auxiliary power unit & start
controller
Electrical power generating &
start system
Primary power distribution
Remote power distribution units
Ram air turbine emergency
power system

Goodrich
Proximity sensing system

Kidde Technologies
Fire protection system

Labinal
Wiring

Honeywell
Exterior lighting

Goodrich
Exterior lighting

Goodrich
Fuel quantity indicating system

Parker Hannifin
Hydraulic subsystem

FR-Hi Temp
Pumps and valves

Source: Boeing
Artwork: Boeing, Juanita Franzi

Rolling along

Boeing announced in early March 2004 that Messier-Dowty, part of the Snecma Group, had been selected to supply the four-wheel main and twin-wheel nose landing gear structures for the 787.

Messier-Dowty was the surprise winner in the contest which had been held against tough competition from Goodrich, Boeing's long-term undercarriage supplier. It was also the French-based company's first win on a Boeing commercial aircraft, Messier-Dowty being better known as a gear supplier for every Airbus model.

Although it supplied significant parts for the 777 undercarriage through subcontracting, its name was more closely associated with military aircraft including the Boeing F/A-18 Hornet, AV-8B Harrier, T-45 Goshawk and Bell/Boeing V-22 Osprey.

In another first for any Boeing commercial jetliner, Messier-Dowty was handed total responsibility for the design, development, testing and manufacture of the landing gear structure, and immediately began working with Boeing to define the gear and the aircraft interface and integration requirements, leading towards aircraft firm configuration in 2005.

As part of combined efforts to drive down operating costs, Messier-Dowty was also a member of the 787 joint Life Cycle Product Team (LCPT). This combined experts from design, test, operations and customer service, to consider all aspects of the landing gears through the life of the aircraft.

Design work involved Messier-Dowty's design teams in both North America and Europe, including assignment of engineers to Boeing to provide support to the customer's aircraft integration team. As with other elements of the overall design work, Dassault's CATIA V5, the latest standard in design tools, was used throughout the process. Meanwhile, testing of the gears was planned at the company's test and development centers in Gloucester, UK, and Toronto, Canada.

Messier-Dowty Engineering Director Jean-Pierre Ferey said the winning bid revolved around "various proposals on weight, cost, environment, new materials and geometries. We put several options on the table, from which Boeing chose the package it wanted." Ferey added that Boeing remained closely involved in the design process through its advanced manufacturing research center in Sheffield, UK. Deliveries of the first of up to 1,300 landing gear sets potentially covered by the contract, were due to commence in 2007.

Later in 2004, Boeing subsequently selected Goodrich and Messier-Bugatti as rival suppliers of an all-new electric brake system, marking the first time a large commercial aircraft would use electrics in place of hydraulics for brake actuation. The decision to adopt electric

Messier-Dowty displayed its 787 undercarriage for the first time at the Paris Air Show in June 2005.
Mark Wagner / aviation-images.com

brakes was taken late in the design process, the system having been originally designed conventionally. Until the 787, the largest electric brake application had been on the Northrop Grumman Global Hawk, an unmanned air vehicle which used the Goodrich system.

Both companies were contracted to compete for the wheels, electromechanically actuated carbon brakes and the electronics that drove the digitally controlled brakes. Predicted benefits included lower weight, increased modularity, more precise control, higher reliability and more predictable maintenance. Brake wear, for example, could be sensed for the first time with the all-digital system, making it far easier to predict when and where to schedule replacement.

Hamilton Sundstrand displayed its 787 common motor start controller, remote power distribution unit and a variable frequency starter generator at the Paris Air Show in 2005.
Mark Wagner / aviation-images.com

Under pressure

Although Boeing had eliminated pneumatics, it did not believe the state-of-the-art in electric technology was sufficiently mature to replace hydraulics.

It decided, however, that the subsystem could be significantly updated and operated at 5,000 pounds per square inch (psi), compared to the traditional commercial aircraft system pressure of 3,000 psi.

Airbus had taken a similar tack with the A380, knowing that the greater rate of pressure reduced the size of equipment needed, thus reducing the weight of the subsystem. In the case of the A380, the change enabled much easier movement of extremely large surfaces, whereas in the 787, the higher pressure system was aimed at reducing weight and improving efficiency. Only one previous commercial aircraft, the Anglo-French Concorde, had been equipped with a similar high-pressure hydraulic system which – in the case of the supersonic airliner – was 4,000psi.

Boeing awarded the hydraulic system contract to Parker Hannifin, which had set up a team to work with Boeing on the definition and specification of the hydraulic subsystem, as well as in its design and integration with the aircraft's surrounding systems. Parker's Abex Division, located in Kalamazoo, Michigan; Air & Fuel Division, based in Irvine, California; and, Stratoflex Products Division, headquartered in Fort Worth, Texas, were all designated to provide components for the subsystem, including pumps, reservoirs, filter modules, associated sensors and flow control devices. All three divisions were part of Parker Aerospace Group.

Parker's Nichols Airborne Division, located in Devens, Massachusetts, and Elyria, Ohio, was selected by Hamilton Sundstrand Corporation to supply liquid cooling pumps and reservoirs for its air management system on the 787. The company's "pump packs", which used the intelligent control of brushless, direct current (DC) motor "smart pumps" with fluid expansion reservoirs and filtration in a compact cooling package, would be used to cool aircraft electronics and electric motors as well as provide galley refrigeration.

Hamilton Sundstrand, not surprisingly given its role as primary power distribution system provider, also extended its involvement in the 787 in September 2004, when it was selected to develop the large DC electric motors that would operate with the engine-driven pumps to generate the hydraulic power in the first place.

The French contribution to the program was also strengthened with the selection of Thales to supply the electrical power conversion system, and Labinal to provide up to 60 miles of wiring. Although this sounds like a huge amount of wiring, Boeing pointed out that it was roughly half the amount of wiring used on aircraft of equivalent size, only possible "because of its innovative use of new technologies."

The Thales system was key to the more-electric aircraft theme because it provided an efficient, reliable way of converting variable-speed, constant frequency power from the engines into standard voltages for the myriad dependent aircraft systems.

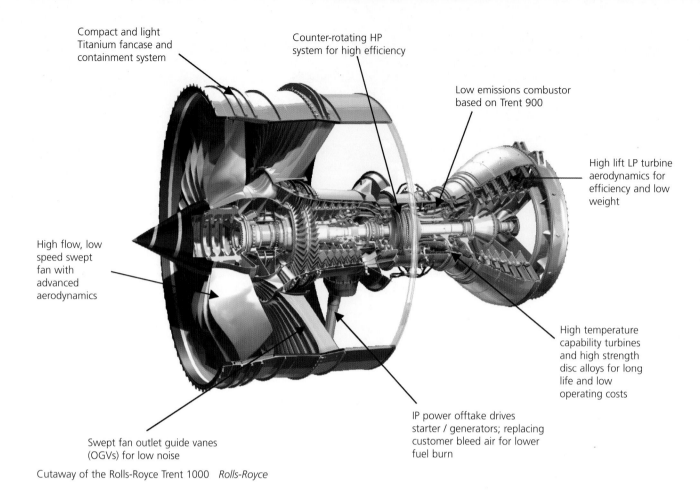

Compact and light
Titanium fancase and
containment system

Counter-rotating HP
system for high efficiency

Low emissions combustor
based on Trent 900

High lift LP turbine
aerodynamics for
efficiency and low
weight

High flow, low
speed swept
fan with
advanced
aerodynamics

High temperature
capability turbines
and high strength
disc alloys for long
life and low
operating costs

Swept fan outlet guide vanes
(OGVs) for low noise

IP power offtake drives
starter / generators; replacing
customer bleed air for lower
fuel burn

Cutaway of the Rolls-Royce Trent 1000   *Rolls-Royce*

Reversing thrust

The critically important development of the extra-large nacelles (the outer casing of the engine of an aircraft) and thrust reversers for the two 787 engine types was awarded to Goodrich in early April 2004. Valued at around $4 billion, it was the biggest single deal ever won by the company which planned to lead the effort from its Aerostructures unit at Chula Vista, California.

The designs were not only large, second only in size to the nacelles of the GE90-115B-powered 777 models, but also incorporated the first ever noise reducing chevron-shaped trailing edge serrations on the nacelles of a production Boeing jetliner. The effort was also split between the two engines, which had slightly different fan sizes and gearbox locations.

The Rolls-Royce Trent 1000 engine was slightly larger than the GE GEnx engine and featured a gearbox mounted on the case. The GE engine, by contrast, was configured with a core-mounted unit. Although Goodrich planned to keep development of the two nacelle and reverser systems "in parallel as much as possible", Goodrich Boeing Commercial Business Vice President Dave Castagnola said the first engine to be launched would mean "putting one application in front of another."

This finally happened in October 2004, when Japan's All Nippon Airways – the launch customer for the 787 – chose the Rolls-Royce Trent 1000 engine to power its planned fleet of 50 aircraft, making it the lead powerplant on the program.

With the decision taken, Goodrich launched into a lean product development plan for the nacelles that also involved the issue of developing a common wing/pylon attachment for both. "It is radically different to anything we've done before," Castagnola said. The company added that the new nacelle design would feature "innovation in the arrangement and architecture" with "split lines and interfaces" different from anything before.

Difficulty is the excuse history never accepts

Global effort

To help it turn the Dreamliner into reality, Boeing girdled the globe in search of partners, to form the most far reaching international development team in the history of commercial aviation.

Unlike the partnerships of the past, in which suppliers made parts and systems to a Boeing design, the new project demanded a far higher level of involvement. This time the players were true partners, sharing with Boeing the responsibility for design and development, as well as manufacturing. This approach meant the costs and risks were also spread more widely, as were the rewards, but it also ensured that partner selection was highly competitive.

Part of the reason for the change in philosophy was the increased technological challenges involved. To achieve the cost and performance targets sought, Boeing had to venture into some unfamiliar territory in terms of materials and systems. Recognizing this from the start, it opted to maximize the expertise of partners which had already earned reputations in their fields for being "best in class".

The partnership concept evolved from the Sonic Cruiser effort, during which Boeing had invited a set of "technology partners" to help with its ambitious structures development. Known within

Boeing as the "big seven", the group came together over the 2001-2002 period as the foundation of what would eventually form a global network of partners.

These included Alenia of Italy, Hawker de Havilland of Australia, the three big Japanese aerospace companies – Fuji, Kawasaki and Mitsubishi Heavy Industries – plus Vought Aircraft Industries and Boeing's Wichita division in the US.

If anyone had been looking for clues as to what Boeing was up to at this early stage, it did not take rocket science to work out that every one of these partners was an expert in large-scale composites manufacturing.

Boeing's goal was to make greater use of composites by weight, a theme that would be carried over to the 787. And to bolster its chances of achieving this, it later invited companies like GKN Aerospace, Fischer Advanced Composites and Stork Fokker Aerospace to join the effort.

For its systems partners, Boeing took the new approach even further. It set up a 787 systems technology team involving 21 companies from five countries, many of which traditionally competed directly with one another. The plan was for the companies to work with Boeing to define the 787 while competing to become suppliers. The team eventually split into several contending sub-teams, all of which aimed to satisfy Boeing's

exacting demands on cost and quality.

In November 2003, the structures partners were announced and, not surprisingly, all were members of the original "big seven". In the intervening year and a half of deliberations, however, it was settled that Boeing should make 35% of the structure, including the vertical fin at Frederickson, the fixed and movable wing leading edges at Tulsa, the nose section and forward fuselage at Wichita, the movable trailing edges in Australia and the wing-to-body fairing in Winnipeg, Canada. Boeing's Tulsa and Wichita divisions have since been sold to Onex Corporation.

The first system partner awards came in February 2004 when Hamilton Sundstrand and Rockwell Collins were selected to provide the bulk of the crucial electrical and environmental systems and the cockpit displays and communications packages respectively.

"Selecting systems partners is an important milestone in our program plan," said Vice President 787 Program, Mike Bair. "We have been engaged in defining systems capabilities at a very high level in cooperation with a large group of candidate partners. Now we can begin to move into detailed development."

Within days, more systems were revealed, starting an avalanche of announcements that would last more than a year.

Super 747

Having chosen a global team, Boeing had to figure out how to get all the pieces of the 787 together on the final assembly line – wherever that might be.

Through 2003, Boeing held a tough contest to see where the Dreamliner would take shape. Sites were considered outside the country as well as all over the US, including Alabama, California, Colorado, Kansas, Texas and Washington. Bair confirmed that studies included more than one final assembly line. "We haven't ruled out multiple sites," he said. "It could give you protection from geographical and political issues."

Along with a moving line concept, Boeing saw the assembly being highly modular in a similar way to the Joint Strike Fighter. "We are talking about a small number of large pieces," said Bair, who added that the eventual plan was to put the whole aircraft together in a remarkably short three days!

The "light assembly" approach, also used by Airbus, involved bringing relatively few, well-equipped sub-assemblies to the final assembly line for mating. This placed the labor-intensive burden on the sites supplying the sub-assembly rather than on the final assembly line. "We have been looking at an assembly line employing 800-1,200 rather than the 3,000-4,000 today," Bair said.

Under the conventional Boeing assembly system, parts arrived by ship, truck or rail, often taking weeks and sometimes months in transit. Boeing knew this had to change with the 787, where speed and efficiency was vital to a business plan. As the "light assembly" depended on fast airborne transport, it also knew the key would be a giant transport aircraft, large enough to take whole sections of the 787 fuselage and wings.

Everett was named as the winning site in the final assembly contest in late 2003, having met the requirements for plenty of available space for the line, a long runway and access to a nearby deepwater port. In October, within weeks of the Everett announcement, Boeing also unveiled first details of an enormous 747-400 derivative that would be the lynchpin of its "Air Logistics System."

Dubbed the 747 Large Cargo Freighter (LCF), the aircraft was unlike any variant of the jumbo ever designed. The upper deck hump was gone, replaced with a massively extended upper fuselage lobe, which extended all the way back to the tail. This increased the interior height by a further 10ft for most of the length of the aircraft, with the tip of the vertical tail being extended to form a slender fin similar to that used on the otherwise short and stubby 747SP (special performance) version of the 1970s.

Wind tunnel tests on the bizarre shape confirmed the taller fin and an upstanding, strengthened upper-fuselage crown beam, called a "strong back", provided sufficient lateral stability without the need for any weird end-plates like those used on the Space Shuttle carrier vehicle. Access to the cavernous interior was via two main deck cargo doors in the aft fuselage, though this would soon change as plans for the LCF came together over that winter.

Brian Bodge (*Front Center*), 787 Program Senior Specialist Engineer, leads a technical discussion between members of the 787 program in the Global Collaboration Center (GCC) in Everett and Jeff Swada (*on screen, Far Right*), a Boeing senior lead engineer in Wichita.
Boeing

787 Structure Suppliers

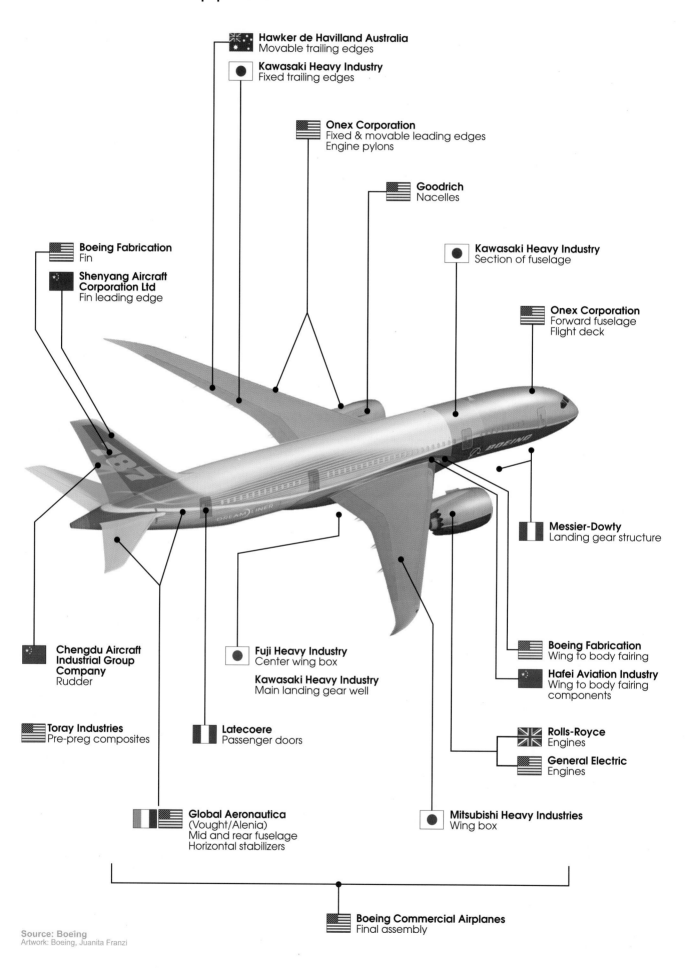

Hawker de Havilland Australia
Movable trailing edges

Kawasaki Heavy Industry
Fixed trailing edges

Onex Corporation
Fixed & movable leading edges
Engine pylons

Goodrich
Nacelles

Kawasaki Heavy Industry
Section of fuselage

Boeing Fabrication
Fin

Shenyang Aircraft Corporation Ltd
Fin leading edge

Onex Corporation
Forward fuselage
Flight deck

Messier-Dowty
Landing gear structure

Chengdu Aircraft Industrial Group Company
Rudder

Fuji Heavy Industry
Center wing box

Kawasaki Heavy Industry
Main landing gear well

Boeing Fabrication
Wing to body fairing

Hafei Aviation Industry
Wing to body fairing components

Toray Industries
Pre-preg composites

Latecoere
Passenger doors

Rolls-Royce
Engines

General Electric
Engines

Global Aeronautica
(Vought/Alenia)
Mid and rear fuselage
Horizontal stabilizers

Mitsubishi Heavy Industries
Wing box

Boeing Commercial Airplanes
Final assembly

Source: Boeing
Artwork: Boeing, Juanita Franzi

Bringing it together

In September 2003, the challenges of putting the 787 together became a whole lot easier for Boeing, when Alenia Aeronautica of Italy and Vought of the US unexpectedly announced plans to form a joint venture to bid for structures work.

The two had already been long-running members of the original "big seven" Sonic Cruiser group between March 2001 and December 2002, and in November the next year were officially named as key structures team partners.

Their joint bid had been made easier by the August 2003 purchase of FiatAvio by Alenia Aeronautica's owner Finmeccanica and Vought's majority shareholder, the Carlyle Group. The joint venture company was called Global Aeronautica and was to be established at a new "green field" site in Charleston International Airport, South Carolina.

Global Aeronautica was set up to join and integrate fuselage sections from Vought, Alenia and Kawasaki Heavy Industries (KHI). The Vought-built fuselage parts, the aft fuselage Section 47 and tail Section 48, would also be manufactured in huge autoclaves housed in a new 300,000sq ft building that was co-located with the Global facility.

The Alenia-built composite fuselage sections would be built in a new 700,000sq ft facility adjacent to Grottaglie airport near Taranto in southern Italy, with manufacturing of the horizontal stabilizer, another part of the Alenia 787 work package, being undertaken by the company's Foggia site.

As part of a $630 million investment, new automated fabrication and assembly machines would also be installed to make the one-piece barrels, beginning in March 2006.

The delivery of the two center fuselage Sections 44 and 46 would start from Italy and go to Charleston in the commodious belly of the 747LCF from early 2007 onwards. The combined sections, accounting for around 26% of the structure, would then be integrated together before being loaded back onto the 747LCF for the delivery flight to Everett.

Between trips to Charleston, the aircraft would also criss-cross the Pacific, picking up loads from Japan, which supplied 35% of the structure. In addition to the forward centre fuselage section, KHI supplied the main landing gear wheel and the main wing fixed trailing edge. Mitsubishi Heavy Industries produced the composite wing box, while Fuji Heavy Industries made the center wing box and was responsible for its integration with the KHI-built main landing gear wheel well.

Shorter flights were also scheduled to Wichita, Kansas, to pick up the Section 41 nose segment which would arrive, as with the other major sub-assemblies, in a "stuffed" state – equipped and ready to put together with the other sections. The overall result was that parts spent just one day in transit to Everett, instead of the average of 30 days seen on other programs.

Meanwhile, Boeing was on the hunt for three 747-400s and an operator to fly its "Air Logistics System". Despite the size of the sub-assemblies, Boeing believed the weight would not require strengthening of the deck on the -400F version. Therefore, the use of former passenger -400s would be sufficient. The aircraft was expected to be certificated by the end of 2006 – in time for the start of the 787 assembly in early 2007.

The modified 747 will feature a swing tail to unload the 787 fuselage sections. *Boeing*

Momentous mod

With the announcement of Boeing's Large Cargo Freighter (LCF) in October 2003, the design team set to work under an aggressive schedule which led to firm configuration being achieved one year later.

The big change was the adoption of a massive swing tail to allow straight-in loading of huge 787 sub-assemblies, rather than attempt to shoe-horn pieces in through side cargo doors.

The volume of the main cargo deck was now defined with an unbelievable volume of 65,000 cubic feet – or three times more than the 747-400 Freighter! The new design meant the entire tail moved around a huge hinge that traced its origins to a similar concept developed by Canadair in the 1960s for the CL-44 – a swing tail freighter derivative of the Bristol Britannia airliner.

Unlike the CL-44, however, the 747LCF tail unit was so massive and its needs so specialized, that it could not be moved using on-board power and required a specially developed ground vehicle to act as a combined actuator and tail stand (see below).

Design work on the upper fuselage, the new Section 47 rear fuselage and the main deck floor was handled by the Boeing Design Center in Moscow, Russia, while the development of the critical "swing zone" around which the tail pivoted, was awarded to

Gamesa Aeronautica of Spain. The award, revealed in February 2005, marked the first Spanish industrial involvement in the 787.

The swing zone added several feet to the aircraft, extending fuselage length to more than 235ft and making it (by just over 3ft) the longest 747 ever developed. The enlarged cargo space was not pressurized and was divided from the flight deck and forward Section 41 by a new pressure bulkhead.

Boeing acquired two of three ex-airline aircraft in 2004 and the third in early 2005. On 18 February 2005, it awarded the LCF conversion contract to Taiwanese maintenance, repair and overhaul firm, Evergreen Aviation Technologies (EGAT). "Modification work will begin on the first aircraft in [mid] 2005," said Boeing 787 Vice President Airplane Production, Scott Strode.

The LCF rollout will be around mid-2006, and certification in late 2006, in time for operations in 2007.

Boeing would rely on two LCFs "with a third to follow later", added Strode. EGAT planned to modify the 747s in its 127,464sq ft maintenance hangar that opened in December 2004 at Taipei's Chiang Kai-Shek International Airport.

Rocketdyne (now incorporated into United Technologies) was contracted to modify Section 41 and Stork Fokker of Netherlands will build the bulkhead.
Boeing is preparing a fleet of massive ground vehicles, which it

will place at the 747LCF's five main stopping-off points around the world to support its flying delivery service to Everett. The largest vehicle, measuring 115ft long and capable of carrying loads up to 150,000lb, will be the LCF cargo loader.

Designed by the same company that developed the loaders for Airbus and its "Beluga" A300-600ST transport, these enormous vehicles will take the sub-assembly and its transport jig directly to and from the factories to the 747LCF. The massive vehicles will be built complete with a "scissor-lift" capability to enable them to rise up to reach the cargo floor level of the 747.

Another set of unusual, purpose-built vehicles is being designed to support and swing open the hinged tail of the LCF. The "tail support stand" vehicle will carry a 17ft high, three-point attachment that will slot into the underside of the empennage. The self-propelled tail support vehicle will then pivot slowly and open up the 44,000lb weight of the swing tail while, at the same time, preventing the aircraft from tipping back during loading.

The first units will be delivered from Canada around March 2006 where they will be tested and evaluated at Everett. On completion of a successful try-out, sister vehicles will be dispatched to Italy, Japan and the other 787 sub-assembly sites in Charleston and Wichita.

The 787s will be assembled alongside 747s, 777s and 767s at the world's largest building in Everett, Washington. *Geoffrey Thomas*

Designing a cyberliner

As befitting the first all-new 21st century jetliner, the 787 was to be entirely designed, tested and even assembled in a digital environment. Not only did this save time and huge amounts of development money but it also ensured a near-perfect design – one that would come together the first time with no last-minute production or assembly problems.

Boeing's first opportunity to take serious advantage of the digital design revolution came with the 777 in the early 1990s when it used a Dassault Systemes-developed design system called CATIA (computer-aided three-dimensional interactive applications). Using versions 2 to 4, Boeing developed what became the company's first 100% paperless airliner.

Unlike the time-honored tradition of drafting the design on drawing boards using reams of Mylar paper, the new system involved designing all parts of the aircraft straight onto the computer screen as solid three-dimensional images. The precise dimensions of each part were stored in the digital brain of the computer which, knowing the same information about all the other parts, was then able to "virtually" assemble them in cyberspace.

If any of the adjacent parts did not fit or some other parts such as ducts or wiring interfered with each other, then the system would flag a warning. This meant these issues, which in the past had only been discovered at the very last stages of final assembly, were avoided altogether.

Not only did this save on expensive redesign work – after metal had been cut – but it also allowed the knock-on effects of adjusting the layout to be understood almost immediately. It also meant the traditional engineering mock-ups,

or full-scale metallic and wood creations of the aircraft, which were built before the prototype was assembled, were no longer needed.

At first, the new computerized process was hard for some of the more traditional die-hard engineers to accept. It was difficult to convince everyone that it was for real. Boeing decided to verify the accuracy of CATIA by building a full-sized mock-up of the nose or Section 41. The CATIA and metal versions compared so well that plans for building a traditional Section 43 fuselage section were dropped and Boeing never looked back.

When it came to assembling the first 777, the parts fitted together so well that the port wingtip was out of position by only 0.001 of an inch! The alignment of the fuselage varied only 0.023 of an inch from nose to tail – less than the normal deformation experienced by the differential expansion caused by sunshine heating one side of the aircraft.

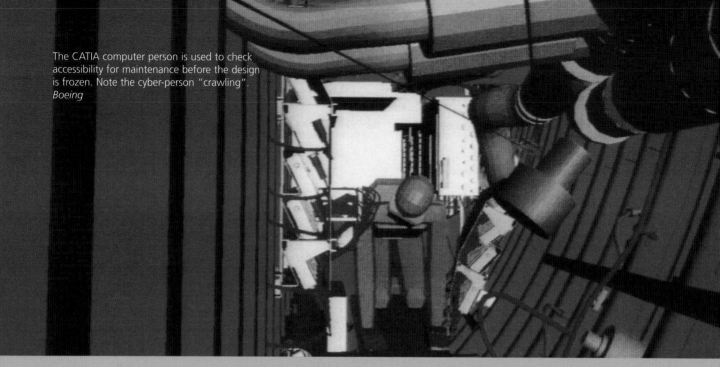

Tapping computing power

More than a decade later, the use of computerized systems was massively expanded to cover not only design of the parts but also their manufacture and final assembly. Design teams were formed and systems were developed to support the 787 in service.

Together with Dassault Systemes, Boeing developed a greatly expanded suite of software solutions to make the 787 a reality. This included version 5 of CATIA and ENOVIA, a software set that enabled engineers from companies all over the world to interface without any errors in translation between different versions. A third element, called DELMIA, was the tool that defined the manufacturing process.

With design going on at companies spanning the globe, the key to developing the aircraft depended on seamless communications between design engineers. Specially-equipped conference rooms, called Global Collaboration Centers, were set up in which engineers communicated using the new software sets in a "virtual workspace".

The system allowed work on the design to go ahead at various sites around the world without a break for 24 hours a day, representing a significant shortening of the overall schedule and the cementing of the team that Boeing described as the Global Collaboration Environment.

Another shift that took the 787 design process a leap beyond that of the 777 was the move to a paradigm called "product lifecycle management" (PLM). In previous programs, the chief design effort was all upfront, and focused on the actual development and production of the aircraft. The service and support aspect was not a part of this process and was generally addressed by separate processes and teams.

Boeing decided the 787 would be the first aircraft it had designed where the life-time support aspects were to be treated with equal importance to the aircraft design itself.

Frank Statkus, Vice President of Tools, Technology and Processes for the 787, was an avid supporter of the new system as head of the company's advanced technology Joint Strike Fighter bid as well as an advocate for the use of one-piece composite fuselage barrels.

Speaking about the PLM, and the related formation of Life Cycle Product teams, Statkus said: "In the past, many good companies designed airplanes. Today, only great companies find a way to develop airplanes using tools to design and service the airplane throughout its entire life, reducing development time and cost and providing the highest-quality and safest product to their customers. That's what is being accomplished on the 787 program."

Designing over the years

Douglas engineers, including Don Douglas Snr (middle front table), working on a new aircraft design at drafting tables in 1923.
McDonnell Douglas

Douglas engineers pour over blueprints for the DC-9 in 1963. *McDonnell Douglas*

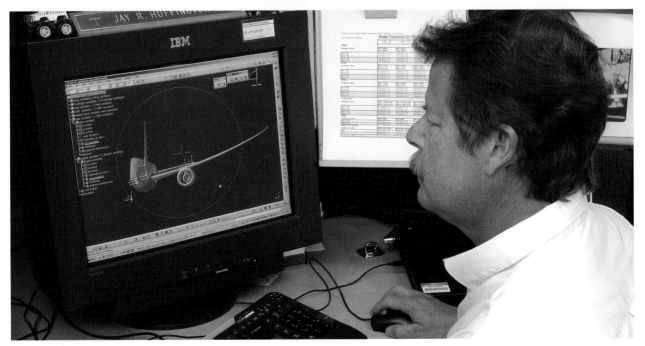

787 engineer, Jay Huffington, works in the paperless CATIA environment. *Boeing*

Speeding the line

Through the late 1990s and early 2000s, Boeing worked hard to develop more efficient final assembly processes that would dramatically lower the cost of each aircraft as well as improve the quality of the final product.

Boeing has gone to a moving line with its 737 and 777 programs to speed up production. Parts for the 787 will, however, arrive at Boeing ready for final join with virtually all systems installed. Final assembly will take just three days. *Boeing*

The basic concept was to reduce not only the amount of time it took to assemble each aircraft on the line but also to cut the lead time from when an order was taken and delivery. By shortening these cycles, Boeing and its suppliers hoped to be able to improve their flexibility and meet the notorious ups-and-downs of the airline industry with their often devastating impact on the profitability of airlines and the industries which served them.

Assembly process improvement initiatives were implemented company-wide, with some of the best numbers coming out of the 777. Flow time, or the time taken from the start of assembly to roll-out, which had started at 130 days, gradually fell to 110 days by 1997, 83 by 1999 and 71 in 2001. Further "lean manufacturing" work brought this down to the low 20s by the mid-2000s, with single-digits targeted for later in the decade.

One of the biggest moves was the transition to a moving line from the traditional "slanted" assembly process in which aircraft were shunted down the line from one "slant" position to another. Inaugurated at the 717 line in

Long Beach the nose-to-tail moving line process was gradually introduced at Renton on the 737 line, and later at Everett on some of the wide-body lines. The moving line concept borrowed from the automotive industry and involved streamlining the process to allow the assembly line to move continuously at a few inches per hour.

For the 787, however, the process was to be different again. Boeing's decision to bring the aircraft together at Everett from several large sub-assemblies meant the sequence could be shorter still. Instead of gradually adding parts and sub-assemblies as the aircraft moved along a line, either in a continuous rolling process or in a series of slanted positions, the idea was to assemble the aircraft in one or two spots or "assembly cells".

To prepare the ground for this, in February 2005, Boeing unveiled plans to move the entire 777 production line to an adjacent bay at the Everett site by mid-2006 to

make room for the new 787 family production line in the 40-25 hall. At the same time, it said the 777 would make the final transition to an all-moving line. The new 777 line area was to occupy building 40-26, the most easterly of the two new bays added to the Everett factory, in preparation for the 777 in the 1990s as part of a $1.5 billion expansion plan.

Although building 40-26 was originally designed to accommodate a second 777 line, advances in assembly processes and the innovations of lean manufacturing rendered a second 777 line unnecessary and the assembly hall had been empty for most of the previous decade.

The final assembly time target for the 787 was meanwhile identified as an incredibly short three days, making it the fastest assembly rate ever targeted for any large commercial airliner and the shortest since the wartime 16 aircraft/day peak production rate for Boeing's illustrious B-17 bomber!

chapter10
These Numbers Add Up

Not everything that can be counted counts, and not everything that counts can be counted.
– Albert Einstein –

Everywhere you look on the 787, there are cost savings. *Boeing*

Operating costs beating them down

Not since the introduction of jet power has an aircraft promised such a dramatic improvement in operating costs over those it replaces. Put simply, compared to the 767 it will replace, the 787 will fly 2,500nm further, burn 20% less fuel, have 30% lower maintenance costs, carry 45% more cargo and it will go Mach 0.05 faster – while offering a great deal more comfort.

And those guaranteed numbers are based on Boeing's ultra-conservative design philosophy. Mike Bair Vice President 787 Program explained that their conservative approach was already evident on maintenance. "In the earlier campaigns, we went in guaranteeing a 15% improvement over the 767 and we're now guaranteeing 30%," he said.

In fact, the 787 has such breakthrough operating economics that its seat mile costs will be equal to those of the A380, which carries twice the number of passengers – a feat unheard of in aviation.

According to Chief Project Engineer, Tom Cogan, this is a huge advantage to airlines because "you get those seat mile operating economics but you only have to gather up 230 passengers, not 550 like the A380."

Everywhere you look on the 787, there are cost savings:
- The composite structure saves literally hundreds of thousands of rivets.
- The aircraft will be up to 15% lighter than those made from aluminum.
- The interior of the 787 is designed to be installed and changed in a fraction of the usual time.
- There are only 30 computers on the 787 compared with 80 on the 777.
- The first heavy maintenance D-check will be at 12 years instead of 6 years.
- Final assembly will take just three days instead of the 11 on the 737.

These, and countless other improvements, have lead to massive cost savings for the airlines in both operating and purchase costs.

Some of the improvements mean that the 787 is 14 tonnes lighter than the A330-200 – one of the industry's most popular and economical aircraft – yet the 787 has 2,000nm (3,700km) more range.

Other advances, according to Boeing's Vice President Marketing, Randy Baseler, mean that the 787-9 with 259 seats (eight across in economy) will burn 4% less fuel per seat than Airbus' latest version of the A350-900 with 279 seats. The 787's claimed advantage in fuel burn over the A350 grows to 10% if an airline opts for the nine across 3-3-3 layout in economy, lifting the seating to 278 seats.

The story is the same for operating costs. Compared to the 787, "the A350 will have up to 14% higher cash operating costs based on a 6,000nm trip with a US airline," Baseler said.

Eddington votes for economy

When Boeing shelved the Sonic Cruiser in favor of, what it termed at the time, a new "super-efficient" airliner – subsequently dubbed the 7E7 and later the 787 – there were many who wondered whether the plane maker had lost the "right stuff".

Sir Roderick Eddington *British Airways*

But in the cost-conscious 21st century, the "right stuff" has the color of money. Former British Airways' Chief Executive, Rod Eddington, who was knighted in June 2005, summed up the view shared by several airline leaders when he told *Air Transport World (ATW)* that "the aviation lover in me wishes it were the other way around, but the airline business person in me believes it is absolutely the right call. We are entirely supportive of the Boeing decision to go for the high-efficiency option over the increase in speed."

Eddington said at the time that "the only competitor [to the 787] will have to be an all-new design – there is no chance of updating any existing design to compete."

As he prepared to hang up his flying goggles and scarf in July 2005, after a stellar career in the captain's seat at Cathay Pacific, Ansett Australia and British Airways, Eddington was still convinced about the compelling economics of the 787 and its point-to-point capability.

"There are at least 400 new city pairs that will open up with the 787," he said. "Our passengers demand non-stop flights and the 787 will be a perfect replacement for our 767s, opening up a host of new city pair opportunities."

Despite the fact that its home base, Heathrow, is slot-constrained for many airlines, Eddington is lukewarm about large aircraft. In the 1990s, the airline cut its 747 orders and substituted much smaller 777-200ERs, opting for frequency. "The logical replacement for the 747-400 is the 777-300ER. We have plenty of time to decide whether or not we require an even bigger aircraft like the A380 or the 747 Advanced," Eddington said.

According to *Flight International* at the airline's AGM in late July 2005, Chairman Martin Broughton, told shareholders that "BA was eyeing the long-range 250-seat 787 as well as the Boeing 747ADV and 777-200LR as possible long-haul candidates. The A350 is unlikely to be adopted as a principal long-haul aircraft," Broughton said.

Some of the 7,000 Boeing employees who cheered the announcement of the record breaking All Nippon Airways order, which launched the 787 (see next page). *Boeing*

All Nippon Airways placed Boeing's largest ever launch order, buying 50 787s. *Boeing*

Customers line up

The first airlines to indicate their public interest were Japan's All Nippon Airways (ANA) and Japan Airlines.

In August 2003, *Flight International* broke the news that both airlines would issue Request for Proposals (RFPs) at year-end to coincide with what was the expected launch date for the aircraft.

On April 26, 2004, ANA stunned the world with a mammoth order for 50 787s (30 -3s and 20 -8s) worth $6 billion at list prices. This was the first time an Asia-based airline had launched a Boeing aircraft.

Starting a trend that has seen the 787 paired with the 777 in some notable orders since, Air New Zealand also set the aviation world abuzz with orders and options for 52 787s and 777s on June 2, 2004.

Then Managing Director and Chief Executive Officer, Ralph Norris, told media at the announcement in Auckland that the 787 was "a game-changer" and that the 777 and 787 would allow the airline to develop new routes and increase frequencies.

Some of the new routes could include Auckland-Denver, Christchurch-Dallas or Wellington-Chicago. Norris claimed that "in selecting the 777/787 family, Air New Zealand has the greatest flexibility in the industry."

Next, with chocks away in July 2004, were UK's First Choice Airways and Italy's Blue Panorama Airlines for six and four aircraft respectively.

At the time, Bair told *ATW* that "Boeing was in talks with 30 airlines for more than 600 787s and had accepted proposals for 100 aircraft from 24 customers."

In October 2004, Las Vegas-based start-up, Primaris Airlines, indicated its intention to order 20 737-800s and 20 787s for premium-class domestic and international services.

Air New Zealand expects to order more than 30 787s over the life of the program. *Air New Zealand*

Japan Airlines ordered 30 787s in late 2004.
Boeing

Airbus moves but 787 orders still flow

In December 2004, Airbus announced details of its A350 – a far more robust and aggressive counter to the 787 than its A330-200 which it had been touting. The twin-engine A350 would tap the 787 engines and combine the A300/A330 airframe with a modified wing.

It would come in two versions – both slightly longer than the 787 with the European manufacturer claiming its higher seat count would offset the 787's operating cost advantage. Ranges would be similar for the standard long-range models.

Airbus was also able to announce its first customer, Spain's Air Europa, which changed from the 787 to order 10 A350s. The announcement and go-ahead of the A350 had been clouded by the heated debate over launch aid by European governments for Airbus aircraft.

Rather than being concerned, Baseler was delighted by the launch. He told ATW that "the launch of the A350 was a great day for the 787." By placing an aircraft on the table, the Europeans cleared the way for real competition. "They can no longer push an all-new aircraft for one airline and a derivative for another. It will make it easier for us to close the business that we have talked about," he said.

Boeing had claimed that it would snare 200 orders and commitments by Christmas 2004 but many airlines were waiting to see what Airbus would offer. The emergence of the A350-900 prompted Boeing to accelerate its 787-9 plans, bringing forward its stretched model from 2012 to 2010.

Airbus claimed that interest in its A350 was high and its commonality with the A330/A320 family was certain to be a major influence on current Airbus operators. With a potential market for 3,500 aircraft over 20 years, the stakes were sky-high.

In mid-December 2004, Japan Airlines gave Boeing a significant morale boost with an order for 30 787s with 20 options to be delivered from 2008. The 787 will replace the airline's 767s and A300s and the airline, like its archrival ANA, ordered both the -8 model and the -3 variant.

Following hard on the heels of the Japan Airlines' success, Continental Airlines placed an order in the last week of 2004 for 10 787s and a substantial number of options. The 787s would enter service in 2009 and operate international flights from the airline's hubs in New York and Houston.

At the end of the same week, Vietnam Airlines selected the 787, announcing plans to order four of the jets to meet expansion plans.

Korean Air ordered 787s as part of a campaign to position itself as one of the world's leading airlines. *Korean Air*

China moves and so does Korean Air

In the single largest order ever placed by Chinese airlines, six airlines committed to 60 787s worth $7.2 billion.

And at the signing ceremony attended by China's ambassador to the US, Yang Jiechi, and Boeing Commercial Airplanes President and CEO, Alan Mulally, in Washington on January 28, 2005, Boeing announced formally that it would return to its traditional naming cycle with the designation 7E7 giving way to the 787.

The breakdown of the orders was:

- Beijing-based Air China – 15
- Shanghai-based China Eastern Airlines – 15
- Guangzhou-based China Southern Airlines – 10
- Guangzhou-based Xiamen Airlines – 3
- Hainan Airlines – 8
- Shanghai Airlines – 9

Boeing will deliver one aircraft to each airline before the start of the Beijing Olympics on August 8, 2008.

Following hard on the heels of the decision by key Chinese airlines to opt for the 787, Korean Air, a long-time Boeing and McDonnell Douglas customer, opted for the 787-8s with an order for 10 plus 10 options.

The order was significant as Korean Air had also enjoyed an excellent relationship with Airbus with 10 A330-600Rs and 19 A330-200/300s in its fleet at the time of the order.

China's six major airlines – *(Left to Right)* Air China, China Eastern Airlines, China Southern Airlines, Hainan Airlines, Shanghai Airlines and Xiamen Airlines – committed to 60 787s in early 2005. *Boeing*

The momentum becomes an avalanche

One of the toughest campaigns in recent times was fought over Air Canada's re-equipment plans for its 767 fleet.

The 787 came out in front with an order for up to 60 aircraft announced on April 25 with Air Canada Chairman Robert Milton, like Norris, describing the 787 as a "game-changer." At the same time, the airline opted for a mix of 36 777s to replace its A330s and A340s as a more cost-effective option than upgrading its Airbus long-haul fleet with premium-class beds.

But the victory was short-lived as the order was conditional on the airline's pilots' acceptance of a new contract related to the aircraft. The pilots, embroiled in in-fighting over seniority issues, rejected the package, although analysts believe the order will be reinstated by the end of 2005.

Analysts predict that the airline will still order the 787 and 777 after the ringing endorsement from Milton, who told media that the 787 and 777 would move Air Canada "into a clear leadership position among North American international carriers with the world's two newest and most efficient twin-engine, long-haul airplanes." He told *ATW* that "our analysis of these aircraft pointed to overwhelmingly attractive economics – the 777 and 787 are stunning aircraft."

And if Air Canada was tough, Air India was one of the longest running commercial campaigns ever, which had its roots back in the mid-1990s.

Air India has suffered from incessant government meddling over the past three decades but a breath of fresh air – which has become more like a gale – has blown through the corridors of power in India in recent times. India is now set to rival China as the fastest growing airline market with Airbus and Boeing both winning major orders from existing and new airlines.

But the Air India order was a win to Boeing exactly one year after the launch of the 787 – April 27, 2005. The national airline opted for up to 50 787-8s and 777-200LRs/300ERs.

After such a long, hard-fought battle, emotions boiled over with Airbus calling for an independent inquiry into the evaluation process, when it alleged that Boeing had been given preferential treatment – a call that was later dropped.

Bair was delighted by the win and said in a global teleconference that Boeing had substantial firm orders and announced commitments by 18 customers for 217 787s, of which 69 were firm. He said that Boeing also had "26 active proposals covering 422 aircraft" and that all production positions for 2008 and 2009 were sold out. Production positions for 2010 had almost reached capacity and those for 2011 and 2012 were filling fast.

Bair also revealed the final configuration of the 787 with the shark-fin tail giving way to a more conventional style to meet aerodynamic and weight requirements. Boeing firmed up its 787-9 Entry Into Service (EIS) date at 2010.

And the good news just kept coming when Northwest Airlines Inc. placed an order for 18 Boeing 787-8s with 50 options for long-haul routes on May 9.

The order from Air India for both 787s and 777s ended tough competition with Airbus. *Boeing*

The competition lifts-off

Airbus' response to the 787 – the twin-engine 250-300 seat A350 – had a delayed start with John Leahy, Airbus Chief Operating Officer (Customers), admitting to media at the Paris Air Show that "it took a while to get it right."

Airbus had moved from a simple derivative of the A330-200 but airlines told Airbus to try harder. The problem was simple. The more capable the aircraft, the higher the development costs and Airbus, with its giant A380 still in development, strove to minimize its development cost burden.

According to *Flight International*, Leahy conceded that the A350, which was launched in December 2004, was the third refinement of the design. However, Airbus was not done with the design even then and up to the June 2005 Paris Air Show put the A350 through three or four more revisions.

While the A350 may look similar to the A300 from which it is derived, Airbus claims it has little in common. The standard A350-800 is identical in length to the A330-200 while the A350-900 is slightly longer than the A330-300.

Both versions have a take-off weight of 245 tons, 12 tons more than the A330. In its 2005 Paris Air Show version, the A350 would feature:

- A new composite center wing box, outer wing box and wing skins
- Flight deck improvements
- Passive and active load alleviation
- Slightly larger windows
- Re-designed interior
- Flight crew rest area under cockpit
- New APU and horizontal stabilizer
- 787 engines with bleed air

Four customers, including Qatar Airways, thought enough of the A350 to place an order for 95 at the air show. This was in addition to the pledges from Air Europa for 10 and the conditional "letter of intent" from US Air/American West for 20.

Airbus has also worked hard on the A350's interior. Sculpturing of the sidewall panels has given a slightly wider (3in) cabin and Airbus has increased the size of the windows, although they are still 64% smaller than those of the 787.

A source of considerable confusion has been the actual passenger loads of the 787 and A350. The seating area is, in fact, almost identical when measured at 50in above floor level – at about shoulder height. However, because of the 787's double-bubble shape and its near vertical sidewalls, Boeing is able to get one more seat across the width than the A350 can accommodate, enabling a 3-3-3 configuration – at 747 comfort levels.

Importantly, said Boeing, the 787 can easily accommodate the large business class beds in a 2-2-2 configuration without compromising on space.

The airlines' interest in the 787's cabin environment pressurization of 6,000ft resulted in Airbus promising a similar capability – at least for the first stage of the flight up to 35,000ft.

Airbus exhibited models of its answer to the 787 – the A350 – at the 2005 Paris Air Show. *Mark Wagner / aviation-images.com*

chapter11
Quick Change Artist

The man who has no imagination has no wings.
– Muhammad Ali –

The drive for flexibility and standardization

Charles Darwin wrote: "It is not the strongest of the species that survive, nor the most intelligent, but the one most responsive to change."

The 787 promises to bring to airlines a new era of flexibility. It has been designed with a clean sheet of paper to incorporate all the lessons of the past 100 years of flight – and airline operations.

Airlines have found one of the greatest drains on profits can be a mixed fleet of aircraft fulfilling a host of different missions. In extreme cases, such as Australia's Ansett, which had seven different aircraft types to serve a mainly domestic market, the complexity can contribute to bankruptcy.

For manufacturers, the battle for simplification revolves around limiting options for airlines, which typically seek a point-of-difference to gain an edge over rivals. But those differences can be absurd. Back in the 1960s, one airline wanted its DC-9s to have cockpit switches functioning in one direction while others wanted the opposite.

Ansett caved in to union pressure and specified that its 767s should have a three-crew cockpit, including a flight engineer, when all other airlines specified two-crew cockpits. In stark contrast, virtually everything forward of the cockpit door is standard on the 787.

By the late 1990s, the airline industry was focused on the enormous cost savings to be made in stan-dardization. It buzzed with claims of 20% savings on purchasing aircraft by shrinking the number of options offered to, and demanded by, airlines when ordering aircraft. The A380 and the 787 offer the first real opportunity for standardization.

But the vexing question for Airbus and Boeing is: How do you sell standardization when carriers are fighting a pitched battle for survival around product differentiation on the smallest items?

As Walt Gillette, Vice President 787 Airplane Development, said: "The financial case [for standard-ization] is so compelling that airline management is directing a change in mindset. The financiers of the aircraft are convinced and that is a major factor."

Boeing is simplifying wherever and whenever it can. For instance, it is eliminating the fuel tank measuring stick on the 787, which has raised some eyebrows, but the reality is that the fuel tank measuring system is 10 times more reliable than that on the 777, Boeing claimed.

"Fewer choices mean fewer options," Gillette said. "On the 777 and other programs, we used a buyer furnished-equipment process and customers had a choice of 16 economy seat suppliers. This process has a 12 to 14-month lead time. On the 787, we are offering six economy seat suppliers and, when the customer chooses, they will get the seats in their airplane in a significantly shorter amount of time."

Another example is cargo doors. On the 767, Boeing offered a number of door options, which proved to be a nightmare because ordering the different sizes was a long lead-time item. "On the 787, we are making all the cargo doors one size. In fact the forward and aft cargo doors are identical and fully interchangeable," Gillette said. He pointed out that the 787 will still have options. "We are offering about 140, which is well down from the 777's 600 but about 80 are just software changes," he said. The 787 cockpit will have just eight line replaceable units, down from 15 on the 777.

For airlines, standardized aircraft are far easier to lease and give airlines greater flexibility to lease in and out aircraft to meet seasonal demands. Critically, standardized aircraft have a much higher resale value. All these factors are significant to airline financiers.

Swapping engines

One of the significant challenges for lessors and financiers of aircraft is the number of engine options offered by manufacturers to meet airline demands for choice.

Until now, the performance, systems, shape of each engine type and critical attachment structure (pylon) for a given aircraft model differed significantly, making swapping engines extremely expensive and sometimes impossible.

Manufacturers have tried to present as few options as possible – but airlines like choice. The answer, which will be a first in the industry on the 787, is to make different engines interchangeable on the same pylon.

Vice President for the 787, Mike Bair, said that this will "offer airlines a great deal of flexibility" and "offer the airlines a great deal of downstream flexibility while enhancing the financing of the aircraft."

As we have seen on page 66, the successful swapping of engines on the 787 has resulted from advances in avionics, where any changes are simply software programmable.

Bair cited the example of the prototype 777, which was powered by Pratt & Whitney engines but, when it came to selling the aircraft, the buyer – Cathay Pacific – needed

Swapping engines on an aircraft from one manufacturer to another can take up to a month but with the 787, Boeing is targeting just 24-hours. *Mark Wagner / aviation-images.com*

Rolls-Royce engines. The re-engine effort took months and cost millions.

It is expected airlines will be able to swap the Rolls-Royce Trent 1000 and the General Electric GEnx engines on the 787 in 24 hours. With the ability to slot 787s into any fleet to meet short-term or long-term demand, the advantages to leasing companies and financiers are enormous.

Bair said that if Boeing achieves what it has set out to accomplish in terms of flexibility options on such items as the engines, bankers have told Boeing that the aircraft will have "a higher loan-to-value than any other airplane, and they see anywhere from 50 to 100 basis points reduction in the borrowing rate."

Interior magic

While passengers will be stunned by the interior of the 787 with its large windows, ceiling architecture and mood lighting, financiers and leasing companies are more interested in the cabin's flexibility.

That flexibility is all about the speed with which the cabin layout can be altered for another operator. According to Boeing's Ken Price, Regional Director Marketing-Fleet Revenue Management, the 787's cabin can be removed and replaced within a day rather than the several days needed for other aircraft. This involves taking out all the overhead luggage bins, toilets and even galleys.

On the 787, an airline will have the ability to change the configuration overnight to meet different seasonal market requirements or weekend leisure demand. For leasing companies, it eases the transfer of aircraft from one fleet to another. The savings in flexibility, according to Bair, are "endless".

One of the keys to this flexibility is the 787's wireless In-Flight Entertainment System (IFE) that will do away with countless miles of wiring to seats, reducing weight and complexity.

Typically, a change in configuration of aircraft requires many hours of painstaking rewiring of seats. In the 787, wiring for the Flight Attendant call buttons has been simplified with re-measured quick-disconnect wires.

Real perspective on the complexity of the wiring for IFE was given by Sir Richard Branson, who found that when his airline wanted to upgrade its 747-200s with IFE, it was cheaper to buy factory-new 747-400s with the IFE system already installed.

Another element is the introduction of LED lighting technologies, which give more reliable and robust lighting systems, greater flexibility in installation maintenance and a much wider range of lighting effects. Also, LEDs, unlike fluorescent lighting, do not generate radio interference.

Mike Bair, Vice President 787 Program, shows the 787's large bins to Mr Song Chaoyi, Deputy Director General, Transportation Dept, National Development and Reform Commission (NDRC), and Mr Liu Wanming, Deputy Director General, Planning, Finance & Development Department, General Administration of Civil Aviation of China (CAAC). *Boeing*

Blue Panorama Airlines' network structure and mix of scheduled and charter flights demands the maximum versatility. *Boeing*

Airline versatility

Versatility of an aircraft translates into versatility for an airline and more profit upside. The 787 is unique in the industry, with its engine-swapping capacity, cabin-configuration flexibility and range capability.

On a day-to-day basis, airlines may, for the first time, consider major cabin configuration changes as an operational option. An airline can have a 787 configured for a larger business class during the week and an all-economy arrangement for the weekend.

Some domestic airlines used to do this with convertible seats that would transform from three-seaters to two wider seats.

However, in recent times, the differences in cabin layout are substantial, which precludes this option.

Bair suggested one of the greatest areas of flexibility on the 787 is its range and size. "It's a phenomenal value proposition and that capability makes it flexible," he said. "We have carriers looking at it in Japan for short-range missions, we've got people looking at flying 5,000nm missions. Other carriers are looking at routes like Shanghai-Detroit. That capability leads to flexibility that the airlines have never seen before. And the flexibility comes from the fact that this sort of range capability was previously only found in much larger aircraft."

Bair said that a great example is an airline like Northwest, which operates 747s from its Detroit and Minneapolis hubs to Narita and a sub-fleet of 757s to beyond destinations such as Seoul. "With the 787, they will just operate Detroit–Seoul non-stop," he said.

"The versatility of the 787 is changing business models. The spread of customers that are interested in this aircraft is right across the spectrum. There are big guys, little guys, charter operators and I have a sneaking suspicion that there's a reasonable chance that the largest 787 operator doesn't exist today. Somebody's going to figure out a way to use this airplane that will be novel to us all. It always happens when you have something that's so unique in its capability – something happens that surprises all of us."

Leaning the lessors

Not only is the 787 a game-changer from a versatility aspect, its genesis is unique in that Boeing has sought from the outset to design the aircraft to achieve maximum flexibility and downstream value for lessors and bankers.

For decades, Boeing has sold airplanes to airlines outright, and more recently, to leasing companies. Responding to airlines' needs was a fundamental of the business of building airplanes, which resulted in a proliferation of options, as we have discussed.

However, with airlines more likely to lease aircraft today, financial institutions have become critically important to the business case. Bair said that Boeing had never really thought much about financing of the aircraft, "which was something the airlines arranged on delivery."

With financial institutions playing a pivotal role, Boeing set about designing the aircraft from the start to maintain its value throughout its life – no matter how many times it changes hands.

Bair predicts the 787 will hold its value better than any other Boeing airplane or any airplane in history.

"There is no question in my mind because of the fact that we're getting input from all the stakeholders – airlines, bankers and lessors," he said.

There is no doubt that the types of materials and the open architecture of the systems on the 787 will help it hold its value. Bair explained that "you can keep an airplane safe and flying for many, many years but the problem comes when it gets too expensive to maintain and operate. That's when it's better to make the investment in something that's better." The extensive use of composites, with excellent longevity properties, is a critical contributor to reduced maintenance.

For lessors and bankers, a major challenge in retaining value in aircraft has been the rapid progress in avionics and the high cost of upgrading aircraft, which were not originally designed for upgrades. Bair said that the open systems architecture that is being used will allow for continual updates of the 787. "The system we are using is better and less expensive," he said. "As more reliable systems come along, we can more easily incorporate them into the airplane and keep it a fresh product for a long time."

Because of the complications of options in 1966, DC-8s were leaving the production line with 25,000 hours of unfinished work. *Boeing*

Mainstream systems

While it sounds like a logical strategy, for a host of historical reasons, aviation materials and systems have evolved well away from mainstream industry.

As we have seen, the 787 will dispense with "boutique" aerospace technologies in favor of open systems and standardization, to help slash operating and capital costs.

Gillette said: "Boeing needs to take the 787 into the mainstream of industry." Composites, for example, are used widely throughout industry, while aluminum alloys are used only by the aerospace industry – at a premium.

Options are also on the hit list. Boeing and Airbus executives reel in horror when mention is made of the number of 747 options: 39 clipboard options for the cockpit, 101 shades of white paint or a staggering 126 lavatory options. According to Bair, "standardization is one of the keys to making the 787 more affordable."

Simplification is also critical to smooth-flowing production lines. In 1967, the famous Douglas Aircraft Company was forced to merge with McDonnell Aircraft Company after a rapid build-up in aircraft orders with myriad airline options. This combined with a parts shortage to hopelessly snarl its production lines. At one stage, DC-8s were leaving the production lines with 25,000 man-hours of unfinished work.

More recently, in 1997, Boeing was forced to stop the 737 and 747 production lines for a month because of parts shortages due to a rapid production build-up. The result was a $4 billion write-off.

That fiasco resulted in the "lean production" initiative – with spectacular results. The time to build a 737 has been cut by 30% and inventory levels of parts are down 42%.

A similar program across the aerospace giant has produced more startling results with production defects down by 90% on the F/A-18 fighter and the number of hours to build an Apache helicopter slashed by 54%.

With the 787, Boeing expects to achieve a 30-40% reduction in manufacturing assembly time compared with the 777, partly because of reduction in airline options.

But aircraft manufacturers still face pressures for a multitude of options from airlines, which design what they consider is the perfect aircraft (interior) but it does not always suit others.

Flexibility and simplicity

The business case is irresistible and simple! Boeing, banks, leasing companies and airlines want to build, finance, lease and operate airplanes that are simple to build, hold their value, are easy to lease between airlines and are cheaper to operate.

In the late 1990s, airlines in large alliances were all abuzz with claims of up to 20% savings on aircraft purchasing by slashing options and buying in bulk. But until now, progress has been slow.

Today, with airline yields diminishing, the need for standardization and simplification is more pressing than ever but many airlines have been caught in a culture of "we have always done it this way."

According to Qantas Executive GM Engineering Technical Operations and Maintenance David Cox, Qantas underwent a radical culture change on the use and specification of its aircraft and the effects of these on day-to-day operations.

"We once had a narrow view of the use of an airplane but today we consider a much greater range of factors," Cox said. "When we review an option or upgrade, it must be signed off by a committee. There must be an excellent business case and it must be [able to be] retrofitted, which precludes most options."

Boeing has also had a much broader view of who it sells airplanes to, according to Bair. "We are now treating Citigroup, Credit Lyonnaise and the Bank of Scotland as customers," he said. "They've influenced the design of the airplane and we have changed things in the design of the airplane to suit their demands. The ability to swap engines was absolutely, solely, done for the financial community."

The financial community told Boeing that if it followed through on its "wish list" of changes, it would see a higher loaned value on this airplane than on other airplanes.

According to Bair "what is also driving the simplification and value case for Boeing is the fact that most of its customers, with some notable exceptions, have on average made no money. So anything that we can do to change that equation is really important."

And there are a host of changes in the business case for the 787, Bair claimed. "Our 787 service package brings an enormous economy of scale to the maintenance of the airplane," he said. "Normally, airlines buy airplanes and buy all the infrastructure and spares to support them, wasting billions and billions of dollars.

"Now we have not only a new airplane but a radically different one with new systems – and nobody has invested any money in the infrastructure. We have the opportunity to offer our services package that allows us a huge economy-of-scale opportunity."

Vietnam Airlines has evolved as one of Asia's fastest growing airlines with a fleet of A320s, 767s and 777s. Its four 787-8s will be delivered in 2010.
Boeing

chapter12
Maintaining the Dream

*Every great advance in science has issued from a new
audacity of imagination.*
— John Dewey —

The 787's industry low maintainability will help ease the pressure on First Choice Airways' demanding schedules.
Boeing

Counting the cost

Boeing set out with as much energy to establish a new paradigm with the maintenance costs of the 787 as it did with the systems, structures and engines.

Maintenance costs are a significant part of the overall costs of owning and operating any jetliner. Based on a typical 3,000nm trip, the average operating cost "pie" can be sliced into specific sections with the largest slice, some 38%, being taken up by the cost of actually owning the aircraft.

Crew costs take up the second biggest chunk with 25%, of which 15% is usually flight crew and 10% is cabin crew. Fuel expends up to 12%, although throughout 2005, this was threatening to creep up as aviation fuel costs continued to soar.

Ground handling costs added 4%, control and communications fees some 6% and landing fees and hull insurance together accounted for around 6%.

The remaining 9% is usually maintenance costs, which are amortized over the years in service and several levels of checks ranging from daily line-servicing, regular base (C-check) maintenance and

heavy (D-check) maintenance. The D-check, in particular, ranks as the most expensive single event in the life of an airliner, other than the day it is formally procured by the owner. The longer and more frequent the maintenance checks, the less revenue the aircraft earns and the more it costs to operate.

If it could attack this cost, Boeing believed it would make a massive impact on not only the operating costs of the 787 but also the residual value of the aircraft to both airline operators and lessors. The maintenance question also linked closely to reliability and, therefore, to availability. "For the first time, we've added airplane availability to this equation," said 787 Deputy Chief Mechanic Justin Hale. "We asked ourselves: For the life of this aircraft, how does the design affect aircraft availability?"

The position of Hale as a Boeing-appointed "mechanic" to the 787 program spoke volumes for the way the manufacturer was now addressing the maintenance question. First created for the 777 program, the position of Chief Mechanic put Hale in an unusual position within Boeing. "I am the customers' advocate," he said. "I work with them to understand their needs and bring their experience back into the program. It's a fantastic job."

Dreamliner targets

Boeing believed its built-in reduced maintenance plans for the 787 could result in several million dollars of additional operating revenues per aircraft over the first eight years of service.

More specifically, it predicted that over the first eight-year period, the reduced maintenance burden would free up the aircraft for significantly more flights than a new Airbus A330 over the same period. "The 787 would have 14 fewer line checks, two fewer base (C) checks and one less structural (4C) check," Hale said.

The largely composite structure was designed such that the 787 would not require its first heavy maintenance (D) check until its 12th year in service compared to eight for the 777, six for the 767 and A350 and five for the A330. The first base maintenance check would occur at 36 months, or twice the interval for the 767/A330. By comparison, the same interval for the 777 is 24 months. Viewed another way, Boeing predicted the 787 would be available for nearly 100 additional flights over eight years when compared to a competing 767, A330 or A350.

Line maintenance check intervals were extended with the 787 at a planned 1,000hr compared with 600hr for the 777, 700hr for the A330 and 500hr for the 767. In addition to the savings on the "A" check improvements, Boeing estimated the better availability from the increased "C" and "D" check intervals meant the 787 would experience around 80% less "downtime". Hale calculated that over an average eight-year period, an airline operating an A330 would lose an average of 122 flights to scheduled maintenance, technical problems and diversions or turn backs in midair. "A 787 over the same period would lose just 24 flights," he said.

What was even more startling was that Boeing was prepared to back up its promises by issuing an unprecedented maintenance "guarantee" to the operators. The company was prepared to guarantee 787 operators a 30% cost saving over the A330 after 12 years of operation – or until the first D check.

"We have got to design enough durability into that structure to go 12 years between major inspections," Hale said. Like all aircraft, the predicted maintenance costs of the 787 "will ramp up over time," he added. "However, the differences we see for the 787 are in the shape of that curve. The age-related maintenance costs for the 787 will escalate at less than half the rate of its metallic competitors. We expect it to undergo a more graceful ageing process."

Minimal downtime is essential for Icelandair, which ordered two 787s in February 2005. *Boeing*

The key to low-cost dreams

So how do you slash maintenance costs so dramatically? The answer, in large part, lies in Boeing's key decision to adopt composites for the primary structure of the 787.

Not only do composites weigh less but they have two inherent properties that make them good news from the maintenance perspective: they have far better resistance than aluminum to fatigue (or the formation of cracks) and they do not corrode. These properties produce immediate benefits when it comes to the number and extent of regular checks that have to be performed on an aircraft to ensure safety.

"When the structure does require inspection, for the most part it will be a visual inspection," Hale said. "People think that because we are dealing with composites, expensive, time-consuming and non-destructive inspection methods will be required. However, because of the type of composites we're using, the vast majority of the structure will require only visual inspection."

The composite material used in the 787 structure is designed with two key properties, which enable a massive reduction in maintenance requirements. The first is inherent to the nature of the solid-laminate material. That is, if damage is undetected and therefore un-remedied, the defect will not grow.

Secondly, damage that is small enough that it is not easily detected visually will not reduce the capability of the structure to an unsafe level. The outcome of these characteristics is that small undetected areas of damage – which may never be found during a visual inspection – are acceptable for the life of the airplane because they will never grow into a larger problem.

This is quite different from metal structures where aircraft maintenance programs are tailored to detect and fix damage that, if left untreated, could reduce strength to critical levels leading to fatigue failure. Aside from fatigue, the primary damage concerns for the standard aluminum-built aircraft are impact damage from accidents and corrosion.

It is, perhaps, this latter area where the 787 is expected to be the big winner. It is a simple fact of life that all metals, including even the most advanced alloys used in today's aircraft, will return to their natural constituents if the right conditions exist. Alloys will break down into metallic compounds such as hydroxides, oxides or sulfates given half the chance, and in conventionally built aircraft there are plenty of these.

For corrosion to happen, an electrical circuit has to be established between the metal and whatever is coming into contact with it. The circuit is formed by an electrolyte – or any solution that conducts electrical current and contains positive and negative ions. In an aircraft, this could be something as simple as a wet or damp surface in the belly containing dissolved dirt, salt or engine exhaust gases.

Ethiopian Airlines was the first to bring jet transport to Africa and has ordered 10 787s for delivery from 2008. *Boeing*

Corrosion – the mechanic's nightmare

Classic enemies of metallic aircraft include galvanic corrosion when two dissimilar metals make contact with one another in the presence of an electrolyte, or concentration cell corrosion, in which foreign material can lead to the internal breakdown between metal joints.

Others include "fill form" corrosion, which attacks aircraft skin beneath painted surfaces, metal ion concentration cell corrosion and inter-granular corrosion, which begins along the boundaries of chemically different parts within the metal and which, if left unchecked, can lead to catastrophic failure.

Corrosion often attacks in well-known areas of an aircraft. By designing for this upfront, Boeing believes it will have the upper hand in the maintenance battle. The use of composites around lavatories and galleys will alleviate traditional problem areas where waste products, food and moisture often tend to accumulate, providing fertile ground for corrosion. As bilge areas all over the aircraft, including under lavatories and galleys, are classic problem areas, the presence of an all-composite fuselage structure is expected to be critical to lowering maintenance concerns.

Bilges act as collection points for everything from waste oils, hydraulic fluid and water to dirt or debris. Worse still, oil can hide water that settles to the bottom of the bilge area, concealing potential corrosion. Drains can also be problem areas when they become clogged with debris or sealants or if the aircraft is not in a level position. With so many potential corrosion areas eliminated from the start, it appeared that Boeing's approach had logic on its side.

Another cost-cruncher is the inherent maintenance savings in the systems architecture itself. "We do not have a bleed system to worry about because we're getting rid of the pneumatics architecture completely," Hale said. "Aircraft pneumatic systems are, by nature, inefficient. They are notoriously problematic and they are very expensive to maintain. Eliminating the engine bleed system from the 787 disposed of the massive pre-cooler, which robbed a huge amount of energy from the bleed air as it left the engine. It made for a simpler, more reliable APU and engine-start system. It also eliminated hundreds of feet of ducts and dozens of valves, all of which had to be monitored for overheating and leaks."

"The integrated drive generators, mounted on current engines to generate electricity for the aircraft systems of today, depend on specific frequencies and rely on a constant speed drive unit which is the weak link in that system," Hale said. "We are going to a variable frequency system [see page 71], which significantly simplifies the architecture. Simplicity is one key strategy to reduce maintenance costs on the 787," he added.

Rubbing out ramp-rash

It happens every day at airports all over the world. Someone, somewhere, will accidentally drive a vehicle on the ramp into the side of a perfectly serviceable aircraft with a resulting expensive crunch.

Nicknamed "ramp-rash" by the industry, accidental damage to aircraft, airport structures and ground service equipment costs the global airline industry a staggering $3 billion annually in uninsured losses. To put it another way, the equivalent cash would pay for around 25 787s every year!

Not surprisingly, Boeing was keen to reduce this cost. "We're designing it [the 787] to be robust, and we've elected to put a few more plies [of composite weave] in several places to keep it that way," said Walt Gillette, Vice President 787 Airplane Development, who added that in terms of savings on aircraft damage alone, "this will help us reduce the $2 billion per year spent world-wide on ramp-rash damage."

Hale explained that the 787 design incorporates what effectively adds up to in-built insurance coverage against the virtually inevitable ramp-rash incident. "For the first time ever, we are adding extra resistance to damage around vulnerable areas as a life-cycle cost consideration," he said.

The composite skin is therefore being thickened around baggage and passenger doors, service access panels and other areas which have historically been vulnerable to accidental damage. Making the structure inherently more rugged also reduces the potentially massive direct costs of repair and replacing specific parts. A new cargo door for a typical 737, for example, would cost around $60,000 while a replacement engine inlet cowl would set an operator back more than $330,000.

"So what happens when it does get damaged and how hard will it be to repair?" Hale asked. Boeing put massive efforts into developing a series of simple and effective repair techniques to allay the fears of operators, who were worried that the composite primary structure would prove expensive and difficult to patch. "The primary means of repair will remain a 'bolted' repair in which a titanium or carbon-fiber plate is simply bolted in place over the damage. These are not new procedures," Hale said.

However, the company has also developed a series of quick composite repairs that would allow the aircraft to be back in service within an hour and which would keep it operational until its next C-check.

Damage from ground equipment is a constant and expensive problem for aircraft built of aluminum.
Geoffrey Thomas

The Electronic Flight Bag will broadcast maintenance information to ground engineers when the aircraft lands. *Boeing*

Finger on the pulse

As with a human, whose sensory system automatically keeps the brain up-to-date with the overall health of the various parts of the body, the 787 is designed with a sophisticated monitoring network which checks the health of the systems.

But unlike a human, who makes an independent decision on whether or not to take medicine or to see a doctor if they think something is wrong, the 787 will be under the watchful eyes of computers that know what to expect and when to flag a warning if they spot anything amiss.

Thanks to advances in sensing and processing technology, the use of the high-capacity Ethernet databus and the shift to a "more-electric aircraft" philosophy, the 787 will have the most advanced health monitoring system yet developed for a commercial airliner. The system builds on the breakthrough technology implemented on the 777 and is being developed in association with Honeywell.

Boeing is taking Honeywell's crew information system/maintenance system (CIS/MS) as a single package that will provide updates to the crew and ground-based maintenance teams on the health of the aircraft and its systems.

The maintenance system is chiefly comprised of an onboard health management system which acts through a central maintenance computer (CMC). This consolidates all of the maintenance information coming from the airframe and engine systems and then helps to isolate faults.

Just as importantly, it also thinks up ways of trouble-shooting any problems it finds and passes its solutions to maintenance. The information will be automatically transmitted to the airline's operations control headquarters to enable maintenance staff to prepare for the aircraft's arrival at its destination with the appropriate fix, be it a software update or even a hardware replacement.

The CMC and the associated airplane condition monitoring function are software packages that will be hosted in the common core system. The airplane condition monitoring function is designed to set up trend monitoring and screening routines which will allow an airline's maintenance department to keep a longer-term watch on the health of the aircraft.

Using established trend data, the system will be able to predict when certain parts will need changing or repairing. This will reduce the need for airlines to stock massive spare parts inventories, thereby further reducing overall maintenance costs and speeding up return to service.

Data loading and configuration management are separate functions that will also be provided by the maintenance system. The data loader supports the insertion of data loads (operational software), such as flight management software, into the appropriate avionics systems.

The CIS includes both the portable Electronic Flight Bag (EFB), a portable laptop-type device ordered by 787 launch customer Air New Zealand that electronically replaces much of the paperwork required by current flight crews, and a secure crew wireless local area network (LAN). This will be used to broadcast maintenance information to ground engineers when the aircraft lands. Using a wireless laptop (equipped with a Wi-Fi card), maintenance staff will be able to walk up to the aircraft and get maintenance information on and off the 787.

e-Enabling

Like a brand-new computer with pre-loaded e-mail software, the 787 is designed to be "e-Enabled" from the start and ready to plug into a futuristic networked operating environment that Boeing is actively helping to develop, primarily through its Commercial Aviation Services (CAS) arm.

The e-Enabled vision aims to make life easier and more efficient for operators by providing them with the benefits of real-time, digital connectivity. The concept ranges from existing products, such as the Jeppesen EFB and Connexion by Boeing system, to greater integration with a growing host of even wider-scale developments, such as Boeing's Airplane Health Management and MyBoeingFleet services.

From the maintenance perspective, the 787 will therefore be the first new Boeing jetliner designed from the get-go to benefit directly from the e-Enabled initiative. If an operator signs up for the Airplane Health Management service, for example, it will allow the airline to monitor engine and airframe information across the whole fleet in real time.

Engineers and maintenance staff will be able to examine system behavior while the aircraft is in flight, establish if repairs can be put off until the next scheduled downtime, and inform the airline operations center if a fix can be achieved at the destination without disrupting the flight schedule.

Acting as a much larger-scale development of some of the existing on-board sensors already hosted within the CIS/MS, the Airplane Health Management service will also determine if pre-emptive replacement of dispatch-critical components is needed to avoid a failure that would result in a schedule delay or economic impact.

Maintenance and engineering services for the 787 will also be encompassed under the services offered as part of the MyBoeingFleet initiative. Described as the "portal to the world's largest repository of aviation information", it also includes flight operations support, fleet enhancements and modifications and spares and logistic support.

As part of its maintenance content, MyBoeingFleet makes more than 100,000 manuals and more than eight million drawings available to engineers, mechanics and maintenance personnel. The system is being developed to provide maintenance and service documents as well as engineering drawings, standards, repair manuals and component maintenance manuals. Under this innovative scheme, operators will be able to arrange to receive automatic notice of new service bulletins and document revisions.

Other elements of the service include a FLEET TEAM family of products to give operators electronic access to quarterly fleet reports and data on accumulated flight hours, landings, utilization and schedule interruptions through Boeing's fleet reliability statistics information.

The e-Enabled vision aims to make life easier and more efficient for operators by providing them with the benefits of real-time, digital connectivity. And life for the 787 pilots will be even easier than on the 777 (shown). *Mark Wagner / aviation-images.com*

chapter13
Wings for Global Reach

Aeronautics was neither an industry nor a science.
It was a miracle.
– Igor Sikorsky –

Handley Page HP-42 of the 1930s vintage. Cluttered wing and tail construction meant a very inefficient design.
British Airways Museum

History of aerodynamics

Aerodynamics is an exacting science, so much so that some aircraft designs have failed dismally – costing billions – because critical drag calculations were out by just a few percent. Even today, with the use of super computers and sophisticated wind tunnels, manufacturers sometimes get it wrong, with disastrous results. In the early years, aircraft designers employed a great deal more guesswork.

The co-fathers of aerodynamic theory were German Ludwig Prandtl and English scientist Frederick Lanchester, who evolved theories relating to thin-aerofoil, subsonic airflow and its effect on the compressibility of air at high speeds, shock and expansion waves in supersonic flow and the effects of turbulence.

Before 1919, many aerodynamicists believed that thinner aerofoils (wings) were the most efficient structures for the speeds of the era but Prandtl's and Lanchester's research showed that the opposite was the case. This led to the construction of much thicker wing sections enabling aircraft designers to insert additional strengthening inside the wing and eliminate the external wire bracing that was common at the time. This reduced drag and costs.

Prominent in the design of aerofoils was the US National Advisory Committee for Aeronautics (NACA now NASA), which undertook to test more than 100 designs of aerofoil in wind tunnels, eventually publishing its findings in 1933. Designers were then able to choose the wing section they wanted from the database. To this day, wing designs are sometimes referred to by their NACA number.

However, through the 1920s and into the 1930s, most aircraft designers relied on dramatic increases in engine power for performance improvements and paid scant regard to the innovations promised by aerodynamicists. This fact was highlighted at the time by Professor Melville Jones of Cambridge University, who claimed that some aircraft had three times more drag than was required for efficient operations. Today, with aircraft such as the 787, designers look for the merest fraction of a percent advantage in streamlining.

Long ago, Germans and Americans realized the importance of an aerodynamically clean aircraft, when they built such models as the Boeing 247, DC-1/2/3 and the Heinkel He170 bomber. Streamlining came from a variety of design changes, including retractable undercarriage, engine cowls (covers for streamlining) and flush riveting.

Swept wings

During World War II, aircraft only approached the speed of sound during dramatic dive maneuvers. Pilots encountered control difficulties produced by the effects of air compressibility. Little research was undertaken into the massive rise in drag associated with flight near the speed of sound.

Swiss aerodynamicist Albert Betz, however, postulated correctly that swept-back wings would significantly delay the onset of compressibility associated with supersonic airflow. Again, the Germans led the way and by the end of the war, many designs featured swept-back wings. Swept wings were the answer to high subsonic flight speeds but they also brought problems.

It was found that as the angle of sweep-back increased, lift decreased and the effectiveness of the flaps was reduced. The more pronounced the sweep-back, the greater take-off and landing speeds and a higher angle of attack were required. These problems were illustrated in the battle between the 707 and the DC-8. Boeing went for a 35-degree sweep-back for higher speed, while Douglas, concerned about a high landing speed, opted for a 30-degree sweep-back and a taller undercarriage.

Unfortunately for Douglas, the DC-8 wing design had major problems that were costly to rectify. The wing design had never been proven in flight and the wind tunnel calculations were wrong. Douglas had gone to the airlines with speed guarantees of Mach 0.84. The unfortunate outcome was that the wing design fell short on guarantees and the aircraft was limited to a speed of Mach 0.79 to achieve the design range.

Computers have come to the rescue in recent times. Calculations that once took more than three weeks to complete and be checked, can be performed in seconds. An excellent example of the improvements in wing design through the use of computer modeling is offered by Airbus, which claims that its A330 wing is 40% more efficient than the wing of the A300B4 from which the A330 is derived.

And there is nothing more efficient than meeting or beating guarantees, said Boeing Chief Project Engineer, Tom Cogan. "There are very, very few cases where we have not met our guarantees," he said. "And it's because of the rigorous process we use. In making performance guarantees, for example, we have an independent team audit the performance of the engine, the aerodynamics and the weight to make sure that the team is not missing anything – so that we really understand, to the best of our ability, the capability provided by the technology. It allows us to deliver what we promise."

Both the 777 and 757 were 2% better and the 767-200 was 4% above guarantee on fuel burn performance, giving airlines the bonus of improved range or payload or a bit of both.

Famous photo of then Boeing President and CEO Bill Allen's "hand of encouragement" on the shoulder of legendary test pilot Alvin "Tex" Johnson as he strode out in his flying suit, complete with parachute, with co-pilot Richard "Dix" Loesch to fly the swept wing Boeing 367-80 – prototype of the 707. That test flight would sweep Boeing to a commanding lead in the jetliner stakes. *Boeing*

The 777 was the first commercial aircraft designed using Dassault Systemes' CATIA. *Boeing*

Super computers

The 777 was the first commercial aircraft designed using Dassault Systemes' CATIA – and the 787 has taken that process a quantum leap further.

According to Cogan, "CATIA Version 5 allows us to look at more design solutions in a much shorter period of time." Boeing says that the new design suite has an increase in capability up to a factor of 10 using relational design techniques.

Cogan recounts a good example of that capability in action, which occurred when engineers were finishing the review of the 787 tail. "One of the designers made the comment that using the previous toolset on the 777, they may have had the opportunity to look at only two or three different designs in the time we had available. As it was, they were able to quickly look at five or six times that many designs thus giving us more choices to better solve the challenges. You hear those types of stories anecdotally all the time. There really is lot of power in the tools we're using."

But the CATIA design suite goes much further than just design of the aircraft, Cogan said. "It's really the entire airplane team value chain that uses the tools – from requirements definition through the design and manufacturing of the product." Nor does computer design power end there. Boeing "will be able to use the suite of design tools to support the 787," Cogan said. "It's called Logical Single Source Product

Definition and the CATIA V5 suite allows it all to be tied together."

This flows through to the illustrated maintenance and parts manuals. Airlines will also use the design tools through Boeing for special modifications and can examine the implications of the change in CATIA.

When it comes to the 787's sleek contour, the traditional wind tunnel simply verifies the super computer's work. "Once we used wind tunnels to develop a configuration," Cogan said. "Now we use the wind tunnel to validate that the computing tools match physics. We do most of our development using the computing tools with computational fluid dynamics. On the 787, it's more sophisticated. Modern computing codes allow us to optimize the aerodynamics in a way that we've never been able to do before."

Cogan added that "in the 1980s, Boeing took roughly 50 wing designs for the 767 into the wind tunnel and on the 777, we took about 18 designs. But thanks to super computers, the 787 will only need to test about 12 designs."

Collectively, Boeing engineers have racked up more than 800,000 hours of computing time on Cray super computers and 15,000 hours of wind tunnel testing for the 787.

787 Wing Structure

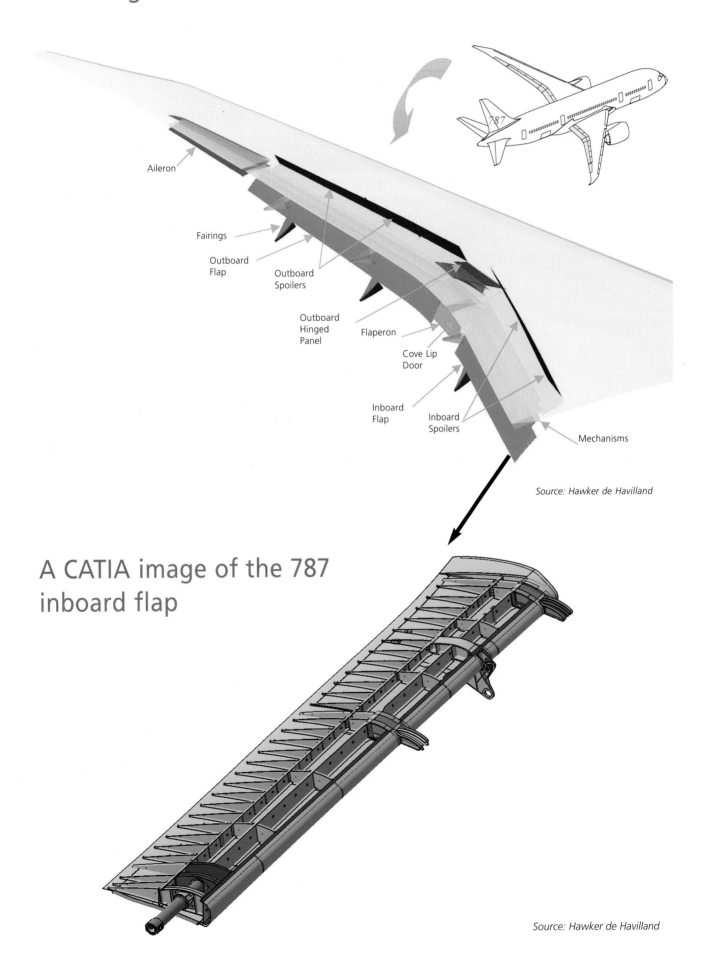

Aileron

Fairings

Outboard
Flap

Outboard
Spoilers

Outboard
Hinged
Panel

Flaperon

Cove Lip
Door

Inboard
Flap

Inboard
Spoilers

Mechanisms

Source: Hawker de Havilland

A CATIA image of the 787 inboard flap

Source: Hawker de Havilland

Gaining the high ground, or higher altitudes, and flying above the traffic will be a feature of the 787. Here, five aircraft cross paths over Romania.
Captain Kevin Tate

To gain the high ground

"Gain the high ground" is the mantra for every battlefield commander and the Boeing 787 will gain the high ground in the commercial aircraft industry with a cruising altitude of 43,000ft.

Cogan said the 787 will climb faster and cruise higher than the 767, which will help keep the aircraft well above most other commercial traffic.

This aspect has become critical for airlines, particularly from South-East Asia, where it has been increasingly difficult to fly desired altitudes over India and Pakistan en route to Europe at peak time – typically after midnight. Air Traffic Control (ATC) congestion over India often requires controllers to hold aircraft at their lower initial cruise altitudes when they enter Indian air space over the Bay of Bengal. Some crews have been forced to accept such altitudes as 27,000ft "for many hours", making non-stop South-East Asia to London flights impossible due to high fuel burn.

Even at a respectable altitude, aircraft such as 747s and 777s, which cruise at Mach 0.85 and 0.84, can also be held up behind slower aircraft such as 767s and A330s/A340s.

The 787, which cruises at the same speed as the 747 and 777, will be able to climb higher than most other aircraft and have virtually unrestricted access to the air lanes, ensuring the fastest flight times. "This all goes back to making sure the 787 can use the point-to-point capability," Cogan said. "We want them to have efficient routings."

Composite wings

Composite wings are not new. They have carried the AV-8B Harrier jump jet and B-2 stealth bomber for years – and seen flawless service.

What is new, according to Mark Jenks, Boeing's LCPT (Life Cycle Product Team) Leader for the 787 Wing/Empennage/Gear Team, is the "nuts and bolts implementation" at a commercial production level.

The B-2's and Harrier's wings were laid up painstakingly by hand but the 787's wings will be built in a far more automated process. A typical wing is constructed by affixing aluminum sheets to aluminum spars with rivets. On giant aircraft, such as the A380, there are more than one million rivets in the wings. Not so, on the 787. Carbon fiber sheets, pre-impregnated with an epoxy resin will be laid up in a mold and then baked in an autoclave.

The wing construction has been undertaken by the Japan Aircraft Development Corporation (JADC), consisting of Fuji, Kawasaki and Mitsubishi Heavy Industries (MHI). A formal contract was signed in late May 2005 detailing their work agreements for the 787, although they have worked together on the project through "memorandums of understanding" since November 2003.

MHI will design and build the airplane's wing boxes – the largest structural elements of the wings. The boxes will be flown to Everett on specially modified 747 Large Cargo Freighters detailed in Chapter 9 for final assembly. "The systems within the wing boxes will be installed in Japan allowing them to be shipped 'pre-stuffed' and ready for final assembly in Everett," Jenks said. Fixed leading and trailing edges, and control surfaces will be fitted during final assembly.

Fuji Heavy Industries will handle detailed design and assembly of the centre wing box and integration of the box with the main landing gear wheel well, while Kawasaki Heavy Industries will provide part of the forward fuselage, the main landing gear wheel well and the main wing fixed trailing edge.

Jenks said that "at this point there are no major technical problems. This is a material that we have used for quite a while now and we understand composites. The 787 wing builds on the 777 empennage [tail] and the basic architecture of the wing box is something about which we have a good understanding. It's really around scaling. The big issue is down to the cost and the processes in the factory – and making sure flow time and cost requirements are met."

"Like the fuselage, the 787's wing is significantly lighter than wings on competing aircraft and it's much tougher," Jenks said. As with the 777 and other aircraft, the 787's control surfaces will all be composite and that responsibility was taken up by Hawker de Havilland (HdH) in Australia. HdH has vast experience in composites and will take this a step further using leading-edge advanced liquid molding composite technology manufacturing.

While MHI and HdH are building large portions of the wing, the design work is being led by Boeing in Seattle, with MHI and HdH designers on site, as well as in Japan and Australia.

The combination of engineering talent and culture is having an enormous impact on the design. Jenks explained that the American style is to attack a problem with gusto, but that sometimes creates wasted effort, although it leads to innovative solutions. "The Japanese approach is more deliberate with careful planning to arrive at a high quality solution. We are getting both innovative and practical solutions." The Australian design approach is best described as a favorable blend of US and Japanese methodology.

HdH's GM Business Development Tony Carolan elaborated on those solutions and said that the use of composites is allowing Boeing to shape the wing design to maximize aerodynamic efficiency to a level not seen on a large commercial aircraft.

Unlike other Boeing aircraft, the 787 will have two wing variants to suit different missions. The shorter-range 787-3 is designed to operate out of smaller airports that may have terminal gate constraints and has been designed with a shorter span incorporating winglets.

The 787 wing will have a common joint for the winglet on the -3 type and the raked wingtip on the -8 and -9 versions. However, the 787-3 wing will be of lighter construction because it does not carry the loads of the longer range and heavier variants.

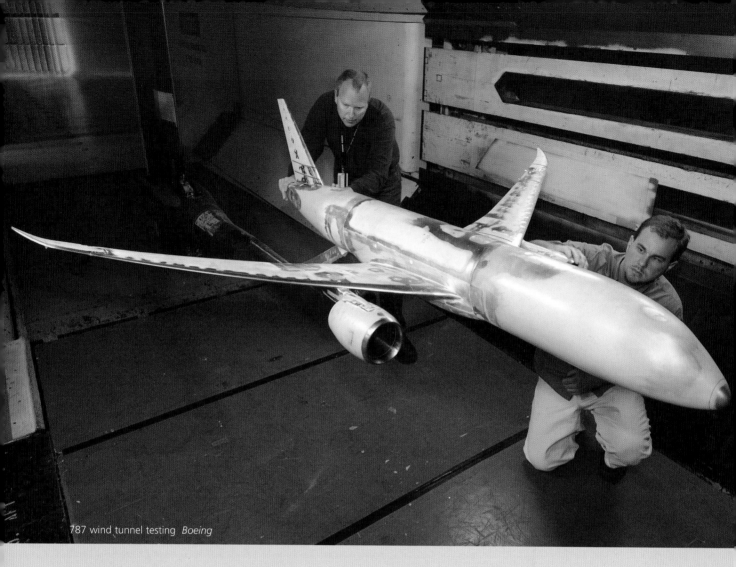

787 wind tunnel testing *Boeing*

Smart wings

The 787's wings will be the smartest commercial wings in the air and build on the vast amount of experience of fly-by-wire control developed in the 777 program.

According to Mike Sinnett, LCPT Leader and Chief Engineer Systems 787 Program, the 787 "takes some of the basic functionality that the 777 has in speed stability and lateral control and expands it substantially." Boeing's primary strategy for the 787 is to have identical handling characteristics to the 777 for pilot transition.

Boeing will also use the control surfaces to shift the loads inboard on the 787 wing during maneuvering reducing the bending movement in the wing, and decreasing structural loading.

Called Maneuver Load Alleviation, it works when the aircraft is maneuvering and the wing is working a great deal harder than in level flight. Sinnett explained that when the wingtip was working 15% harder in a 30-degree turn, there was significant bending of the wing because 15% more lift must be created to stay level.

"So what we are doing is tailoring the lift distribution as a function of the load, to move the load inboard and reduce the amount of work the outboard section has to perform in a turn," he said. This enables Boeing to reduce the weight of the outboard wing.

This is made possible with the use of spoilers, ailerons and flaperons (see diagram on page 117), which adjust the profile across the wing, as well as the sophistication of the 787's fully augmented lateral flight control system.

Sinnett said that on the 787, Boeing has been able to use the same technology to protect the aircraft's vertical fin so that it is never subjected to loads that would exceed the ultimate load capability of the airplane.

*You haven't seen a tree until you've seen its shadow
from the sky.
— Amelia Earhart —*

Downstairs bar on the Boeing 337 Stratocruiser *Boeing Historical Archives*

First Class lounge on an Eastern Airlines Douglas DC-8 *McDonnell Douglas*

Putting pressure on jet lag

It is probably no surprise to anyone that our bodies do not actually like being stuffed into an aluminum tube and shot through the air at 600mph for one hour – let alone for 14.

That tube is pressurized to an altitude of 8,000ft and has extremely low humidity to help eliminate corrosion damage to the fuselage – but this takes a toll on passengers. This is why airlines encourage us to drink plenty of water and to leave the alcohol alone.

According to a comprehensive study into "The Possible Effects on Health of Aircraft Cabin Environments" commissioned by the British Civil Aviation Authority (CAA), some passengers may experience mild hypoxia at altitudes of 8,000ft, the symptoms of which include reduced exercise capacity, fatigue, possible mild hyperventilation, headache, insomnia and swelling of the extremities. While the effects are very mild, they do combine to cause varying levels of discomfort.

The enormous strength and non-corrosive properties of the 787's reinforced carbon-fiber fuselage has given designers the opportunity to eliminate some of the significant factors which cause jet lag. The 787 will have a pressurization altitude of just 6,000ft and humidity levels between 15 and 20%.

How we feel on an aircraft is the result of a multitude of factors, some of which the aircraft designers control, and others, such as seating configuration, which are the airlines' responsibility. With the 787, Boeing's design team set out to "look at all the factors that make passengers more comfortable – both physical and psychological," said Mike Sinnett, LCPT Leader and Chief Engineer Systems 787 Program.

One of the major factors that Boeing controlled was pressurization. Sinnett explained that Boeing turned to the Oklahoma State University for assistance. A study was conducted using US Army Research Institute of Environmental Medicine methodology, characterizing 68 possible altitude symptoms to determine comfort levels at various pressurization levels.

The 500 participants surveyed experienced a 20-hour flight regime in an airplane-cabin simulator at Oklahoma State University pressurized to five different altitude equivalents. Each level was tested nine times. Participants sat in standard economy-class seats, ate typical airline food, watched movies and slept as they would during a real flight.

Participants were selected by gender and age to represent the typical cross-section flying public and they completed surveys before and during the simulation, also undergoing memory, coordination and visual tests.

The results were conclusive. Study participants reported feeling less achy, more relaxed and more comfortable with the 6,000ft cabin pressurization. "We found that there was little difference in the effect on passengers from sea level to 6,500ft," Sinnett said.

787 interior mockup *Boeing*

The 787 windows are almost as large as those of the Douglas DC-8. Here, Don Douglas gives perspective to the size of the DC-8 windows on his first flight in the DC-8 in 1959. *McDonnell Douglas*

The air around you

Robert Louis Stevenson said that "it is not so much for its beauty that the forest makes a claim upon men's hearts, as for that subtle something, that quality of air, that emanation from old trees, that so wonderfully changes and renews a weary spirit."

Aircraft manufacturers are striving to bring that smell of the forest into an aircraft cabin but the complexity of aircraft and their systems – not to mention the close proximity of so many passengers – poses challenges.

"The challenge is to get volatile organic compounds (VOCs) out of the cabin," Sinnett said. "We were really surprised that VOCs,

more than humidity, affect how people feel at the end of a flight."

Sinnett explained that aircraft manufacturers do a good job with particulates (airborne particles) using High Efficiency Particulate Air filters (HEPA) but getting gaseous contaminates out of the air was more of a challenge – but one of real importance. "We looked at the data that came out of the test chambers and it was really evident that the VOCs were contributing more to the people's feelings of being dried out than actually the humidity did," he said.

"VOCs dry you out and alcohol is an astringent. If you consume too much alcohol, this will certainly dehydrate you, but we found that just having the alcohol in the air is a problem – it is one of the biggest components of VOCs in

airplanes today. We even get alcohol from the handy wipes that they hand out at meal time." But it is not just alcohol. There is also hair spray and perfume. So in a world first for commercial aircraft, Boeing turned to Donaldson Company Inc for a new filtration system that will remove gaseous irritants and odors from the aircraft cabin, as well as allergens, bacteria and viruses.

Donaldson, headquartered in Minneapolis, Minnesota, and founded in 1915, is an industry leader in filtration, with systems on aircraft from DC-10s and 737s to the 777. It is also a worldwide provider of filtration systems for industrial and engine markets, including in-plant air cleaning, compressed air and gas purification, power generation, defense and off-road equipment and trucks.

Genesis of cabin layout

We would all love to travel First Class at the lowest discount fare, but until now, commercial reality has dictated a different scenario.

Like all aspects of commercial aviation, cabin design is a battle between luxury and economic reality, with the latter winning out – until now.

The 787 is a game-changer in interior design, just as the 747 was in 1970, and Boeing has again turned to leading industrial designers, Teague, for inspiration.

Teague was founded in 1927 by one of the world's leading industrial designers. Walter Dorwin Teague and his contemporaries such as Bel Geddes, Henry Dreyfuss and Raymond Loewy were treated like film stars in the 1930s. The company has worked with Boeing since 1947 and its first project was the design of the luxurious Stratocruiser interior with its famous downstairs bar. But jet era market realities, with economy being the major driver, have tested designers' ingenuity.

In the 787, that ingenuity has blossomed, as Teague designers have taken the world's most expensive real estate – an aircraft cabin floor – and created a magnificent interior that is impressing passenger focus groups and airline accountants alike.

According to Klaus Brauer, Boeing Commercial Airplanes Director Passenger Satisfaction and Revenue, the floor space on the 787 is "worth about a thousand times as much as the most expensive real estate in Seattle."

"We can't do much with the floor but with the 787 we have overhead space to work with," Brauer said. Boeing has designed the 787 with an oval shape, which gives nearly perpendicular walls, and high arching ceilings allowing designers plenty of scope for innovation.

Sinnett added another perspective. "For the first time, Boeing has gone out aggressively with a specific goal of making the interior better for people," he said. "For instance, at meetings, we are saying 'Sure. We have weight targets… but we've also got [interior] noise targets' – I've never had that before."

The lightness of the 787's composite structure, combined with the enormous fuel savings of its engines and systems, is giving designers more flexibility to add a few pounds of weight to achieve the optimum cabin for passengers.

The 787 interior can be installed in just one day.
Boeing

A cabin of dreams

Vice President 787 Program Mike Bair in the 787 mock-up *Boeing*

Passengers remember their last flight with frustration and their first flight with pleasure – that is the finding of a Boeing study which underscores the philosophy of the 787 cabin.

"We are going to bring back the pleasure of flying with the 787," Brauer said. "Today, passengers have to endure clogged freeways on the way to the airport, a check-in line and then security queues before they get to the airplane door. Passengers feel relief when they finally board the airplane and see the interior as a sanctuary.

"In the 787, we have found ways to enhance the best ideas from the award-winning Signature Interior on the 777 with the latest technology and innovations." That innovation and technology have combined with ingenuity to create a world of tranquility unparalleled on a commercial aircraft.

As you enter the 787, you are greeted by an entirely different cabin with an LED skylight…then you're struck by the enormous windows that bring soft light streaming into the cabin.

The effect? You are not entering an airplane, you have entered a spaceship. Enormous overhead luggage bins consume your huge carry-on bag with ease, freeing the area under the seat in front of you, and no matter where you sit, you can see the world outside.

The 787 cabin is 226in wide – up to 14in wider at shoulder height than the competing A330 and A350 – which, in a standard configuration, gives wider seats and aisles for all passengers.

Entry onto the 787 – a vastly different travel experience *Boeing*

The 787 windows will afford all passengers a view of the world outside, bringing back the magic of flying.
Geoffrey Thomas

Window to the world

What is in a window? Not a lot? Well think again, because it can change your entire travel experience, according to Captain Miki Katz, who flies El Al 777s.

Captain Katz is an international expert in the fear of flying and stress. He has run courses and seminars since 1993. His advice to passengers with a fear of flying is to ensure they sit by a window.

On his website www.airfraid.com, he explained: "Yes, I know it might seem silly, but try it and feel the difference in sitting at a window and looking out as much as possible. Sitting in the aisle can increase the feeling of crowdedness because you see all the rows, all the passengers, but you can't see the windows and your subconscious can raise the

feeling of enclosure and density. Looking out a window reveals infinite open spaces and a feeling of abundant air."

At 19in by 11in on the 787, the windows are so large that all passengers, no matter where they sit, can see out, thus significantly reducing the effects of claustrophobia.

Boeing has been able to add the larger windows because of the strength of the composite fuselage. While the 787 windows are not the largest windows ever seen in a commercial aircraft, the 787 has far more window area. The DC-8 had windows 18in by 14in but they were spaced 40in apart, whereas the 787 windows are just 20in apart.

"Focus groups told Boeing that passengers consistently gave aircraft with larger windows higher ratings than cabins with

smaller windows," Brauer said. "We believe that a good experience casts a halo over the whole airline."

Brauer added that frequent flyers – typically high yield travelers – will quickly seek out the 787 over other aircraft types. "Soon there will be two types of airlines – those with the 787 and those without," he said.

The 787 windows will not have typical shades. Instead, their transparency will be controlled by photo-chromatic technology seen in some business jets.

Flight attendants will control the overall range of the windows' transparency and passengers will use seat dimmers to make individual adjustments. However, the dimming effect will be more like having sunglasses on the window to take out the glare, so window gazers will be happy.

Air Canada's desire to order 777s and 787s has not had a smooth ride with the airline cancelling its commitment due to industrial problems with its pilots. However, analysts expect the order to be reinstated. *Boeing*

Smoother and quieter ride

It is quite certain the famous American poet T S Eliot, did not have the 787 in mind when he penned the words "the journey, not the arrival, matters."

The journey on the 787 is going to be significantly different from any other aircraft, with a smoother ride and a "library quiet" cabin.

The 787 will feature vertical gust suppression for significantly improved ride quality. Sinnett explained that "the 777 has lateral gust suppression with pressure sensors on either side of the tail's vertical fin to sense pressure differential, which actually moves the rudder before the airplane reacts, so the rear of the aircraft doesn't wag sideways.

"In an industry first, we're taking that same concept and applying it in the vertical axis on the 787, so that in essence we can create direct lift control with the spoilers, ailerons and flaperons in a way that the 787 senses the pressure differential that would cause added or subtracted lift.

"By bringing about an automatic vertical response, we can cancel out the bump [caused by turbulence] before it ever happens and the airplane doesn't move. The 787 is going to be the smoothest ride in the sky."

It is not possible to eliminate turbulence but Sinnett declared that, according to Boeing analysis data, the 787 ride will have vertical gust reactions, in some cases, 70% smaller than the size of a corresponding gust reaction on the 777, which is itself considered an industry leader in ride quality. "There's still going to be an airplane response to some degree but it's not going to be nearly as pronounced," he said. "So it's going to feel like the turbulence is a lot lighter than it actually is. We're pretty proud of that."

A combination of the higher bypass engines discussed in Chapter 7 and the latest technology insulation is actually giving Boeing a dilemma. Passengers want some reassuring noises and do not want other passengers overhearing their conversations.

On the 787, Boeing claims it will virtually eliminate irritating sounds from pumps and motors along with the sometimes alarming aerodynamic noises when flaps are deployed. Passengers will just hear a reassuring hum from the engines, suggested aero-engine manufacturer Rolls-Royce.

chapter15
Let the Show Begin

The Wright Brothers created the single greatest cultural force since the invention of writing. The airplane became the first World Wide Web, bringing people, languages, ideas, and values together.
– Bill Gates, CEO, Microsoft Corporation –

Boeing's Connexion by Boeing 737-400 test aircraft
Boeing

Making your Connexion

The 787 will be the first Boeing jetliner to have a cabin designed from the ground up to accept the "Connexion by Boeing", a broadband service which had been in development since 2000 to provide passengers with affordable, high-speed internet access.

"The aircraft will be configured with Connexion as a provisioned option," said Mike Sinnett, LCPT Leader and Chief Engineer Systems for the 787. "So we will have provisions on the aircraft and it will be up to the operator to take it. But we are trying to build the backbone into it."

The system was developed to enable passengers to use a laptop at their seat to check e-mail, to surf the net or even to check their own company intranet. Data flows to and from the aircraft via a broadband satellite-communication antenna which connects to a network of communications satellites girdling the globe.

The antenna was to be mounted on the crown of the fuselage under a low-profile fairing. Although designed to use electronically phased array antenna technology, the system was later adapted to use the more recent mechanically steered antennas developed by Mitsubishi Electronics.

Originally tested on a Lufthansa-operated Airbus A340 in 2004, after flight tests on Boeing's own Connexion 737-400 flying test bed, the mechanical antenna was developed to improve coverage above 65° latitude. The original phased-array antenna continued to be offered for "government" platforms.

The steerable antenna used data from the aircraft's inertial navigation system to establish a rough pointing direction before implementing a fine-tuning "step-tracking" process to lock on to the satellite. In step-tracking, the algorithms in the processor sequentially compare the amplitudes in the signal lobes and, within milliseconds, home in on the satellite by focusing on the zones of maximum signal strength.

The antenna could track down to zero degrees, which meant it could get low-angle coverage at high latitudes up to 80° north. The antenna was designed to be extremely reliable with a time between failure of the system expected to be around 25,000 hours. It was packaged in a fairing measuring around 7.5ft by 3.6ft.

Connexion eventually plans to use its worldwide network for operational uses, such as cabin management and flight crew applications, and it could potentially be used in future 787s as a replacement for systems such as the ARINC communicating and reporting system – ACARS.

The best in entertainment and connectivity will be a feature of the 787 cabin.
Boeing

Connected cabin

From the outset, Boeing was determined to ensure the 787 was the most enjoyable aircraft ever in which to experience a journey. A vital element of this goal was a cabin that was not only comfortable but which could provide the best in entertainment and connectivity.

The plan was to host everything from the very latest in in-flight entertainment (IFE) to Connexion by Boeing and full wireless Video-On-Demand (VOD) capability.

"We have designed it to enable the airlines to keep up-to-date with the latest IFE systems very easily," said Sinnett, who added that this was done with three basic enablers.

"First, we have developed with the IFE industry an industry standard backbone to which any system can be adapted," he said. "It really is 'plug and play' and although that's an overused phrase, it is very appropriate in this case."

The second key enabler was something that can be thought of as a "power stick". Sinnett explained that in the new design, power passed throughout the cabin via the seat tracks. "Instead of having to take these big kits of parts, and prepare raceways and wire bundles, you just have a simple 'stick' with

a conductor built into it," he said. Standard current cabin architectures are stuffed full of copper conductors, which connect to every seat to provide power for laptop computers, reading lights, headset volume, screen controls, cabin call buttons and, in the case of business and first-class seats, the motors that control the position of the seats. "So getting rid of all that was a major technical challenge, and one that was solved with the power stick," Sinnett added.

Changes to the cabin layout, and its associated wiring for IFE and seat power, were therefore made possible by simply pre-kitting stick size to fit the planned seat pitch. "It turns out it takes less than 10% of the time it normally takes to reconfigure a cabin," Sinnett said. "Now an airline will have the ability to change the interior more cheaply and easily and the reliability will improve. And these things take a beating – they get drinks spilled on them and children playing with them, so power sticks will help there, too!"

The changed power supply option also allowed Boeing and the IFE providers to dramatically reduce the size of the large "black box", which was normally required to support the system at each seat. The change, which reduced the size of the box to around 10 to 30% of the current box, not only cut weight throughout the cabin but also opened up significant amounts of extra leg-room and stowage space.

In-flight entertainment has become vital to woo passengers on long-haul flights. *British Airways*

What's showing on your screen?

Just as passengers want better fare options, they also want the maximum in entertainment options on the personal seatbacks, or seat-mounted screens.

This is where the additional connectivity concerns of the 787 design team came into play. "Connectivity is all about how broad a pipe you want to build-off the aircraft," Sinnett said. "You can get a wireless LAN (local area network) in an aircraft for e-mails, or you can have a connection to aircraft off-board systems, but none of the current approaches are nearly big enough to give independent wireless channels showing DVD-quality video at every seat."

The third enabler – the wireless backbone – was expected to not only ease issues of reconfiguring cabins and IFE systems, but also to be far more reliable, lighter and more efficient than current hard-wired systems. "The backbone

consists of antennas that distribute content wirelessly to the cabin, which is much simpler than today's systems," Sinnett said.

The distributed network of wireless broadcast antennae, or "access points" throughout the cabin gave Boeing the ability to project different channels of high-quality VOD, independently to every seat on the aircraft.

Antennas are located along the length of the cabin to cover several seat rows each, providing multiple zones along the length of the aircraft. "We've shown it to work in a variety of cabins ranging in size from the 727 and 767 to the DC-10 and 747 in 'used' aircraft in the desert, museums and in the factory," Sinnett said. "We tried different places for the access points, and different configurations with various layouts of galleys, lavatories and other 'monuments' to see what effect they might have on the coverage. In terms of bandwidth and connectivity, it's light years beyond what we have today."

The basic enabling technology in this case was antenna shaping, which cleverly allowed "channel re-use" or the use of a single channel to distribute several programs simultaneously in different parts of the cabin.

By shaping the antenna in a particular way, engineers discovered the energy distribution could be manipulated to carry different programs on the same channel to different zones of the aircraft. "One person in row 12 will be watching a program on channel 4, and at the same time, another person at row 22 will be able to watch different content on the same channel with no energy overlap, so that the channels don't interfere," Sinnett added.

More recent breakthroughs in wireless broadcast technology, signal formatting and signal de-coding may also be used to distribute on-demand channel content throughout the cabin, possibly augmented by antenna-shaping.

chapter16
Flying a
Super Jet

There's a big difference between a pilot and an aviator.
One is a technician; the other is an artist in love with flight.
— E. B. Jeppesen —

When Boeing moved from an analog cockpit on the 747-300 (shown) to a computerized cockpit for the 747-400 it was able to eliminate 600 dials. *Qantas*

Safety soars

Aside from the growth in size of the engines that power today's aircraft, there is possibly no better visual example of the development of aircraft technology than the aircraft cockpit.

The first aircraft were rudimentary affairs and so were the flying instructions. In 1919, the US Army Air Service, the forerunner of the USAF, listed 27 flying regulations. Number 12 stated: "If you see another machine near you, get out of its way." Good advice!

However, by 1939, on the Boeing 314 Clipper, the cockpit was complex and required a crew of five. Even on the first 707s in 1959, there were two pilots, an engineer and a navigator.

The requirement to have a navigator on board became irrelevant during the 1960s and, by 1981 the Federal Aviation Authority

(FAA) deemed that a flight engineer was no longer required on high capacity twin-aisle aircraft. It was decided that a two-pilot crew was sufficiently safe, due to the advances in cockpit automation and the dramatic improvement in engine reliability.

The extraordinary increase in automation was highlighted when Boeing moved from an analog cockpit with gauges and dials on the 747-300 to a computerized cockpit for the 747-400 with eight-inch Cathode Ray Tube (CRT) displays. The result was the elimination of 600 dials and gauges.

A further example of the advances brought about at this time was the significant reduction in the complexity in crew procedures. On the 747-300, a decompression incident required 20 pilot actions, whereas on the 747-400, it required just 3.

Fourteen computers dedicated to flight control on the 747-300 were replaced by just three on the -400

model and three Multipurpose Control Display Units (MCDU) replaced 11 radio/navigation/flight-data/load panels and 24 dedicated test switches.

Cockpit automation has had a profound effect on safety. The accident record of the 717, which started life in 1965 as the DC-9, gives an insight into the dramatic effect that technology has had on aircraft safety. In 1965, the initial DC-9 had a crash record of 1.26 per million departures (PMD). The updated model, the DC-9 Super 80, later renamed the MD-80, had a crash rate of just 0.43 PMD, while the ultimate version – the MD-95, renamed the 717 after the merger with Boeing – with a fully computerized cockpit has an unblemished record. The 737NG and the 777 also have accident-free records.

The 787 cockpit takes that superb record and goes even further, as we will see. The cockpit is a pilot's dream and bristles with the latest in technology and ergonomics.

Computer-generated image of the 787 cockpit *Boeing*

Extraordinary safety

Boeing believes the 787 will be the safest, most dependable airliner yet built.

Combining the latest in design, systems and structures know-how, it also builds on the countless lessons learned over the years from every previous generation.

All the designers at Boeing and Airbus live with the past accident statistics. "It's kind of tattooed on the insides of our eyelids," said Life Cycle Product Team (LCPT) Leader and Chief Engineer Systems 787 Program, Mike Sinnett. "I close my eyes, look up and see the chart of the number of hull losses per millions of departures. I consider what the primary causes are and how we've brought the primary causes down. We are constantly making discrete design changes to avoid the one-off events that might never ever happen. But we make sure they never happen through design."

All of the hull losses in 2004 were older generation types and one-third of those were approach and landing accidents, including controlled flight into terrain (CFIT). These dreaded CFIT accidents, which in the 1990s and early 2000s accounted for more than half the annual statistics, occurred when a perfectly airworthy aircraft under the control of the flight crew was flown unintentionally into terrain, obstacles or water, usually with no prior awareness by the crew.

A key design imperative of the 787 flight deck was to provide crews with the best ever picture of where the aircraft was in time and space. Known as "enhanced situational awareness", the approach embraced advanced sensors, warning systems and visual aids, such as dramatically larger "flat panel" liquid crystal display instruments and dual Head-up Guidance System (HGS) as standard.

In terms of performance, Boeing established from the start that the 787 would be instrumented to enable precision approaches to be made to all runways. Precision approaches allow an aircraft to be guided laterally and vertically all the way down to the runway. In the past, precision approaches had only been possible for runways equipped with instrument landing systems that beamed electronic signals guiding aircraft towards the runway.

With the availability of satellite-based navigation and the spread of global positioning system (GPS) ground stations, a new and more accurate navigation system became available allowing aircraft to follow specific routings as well as enabling precision approaches to virtually any runway.

In the case of the 787, the target was to stay within 0.1nm of the centerline of a specific track with a 95% probability. This designated navigational performance (DNP) of 0.1nm was the key to not only improved safety but also greater operating efficiency.

Members of the Boeing 787 design team *(Left to Right)*: Walt Gillette, Mike Sinnett, Mark Jenks and Tom Cogan discuss design issues. *Boeing*

Integrated avionics

Unlike every civil aircraft, other than the Airbus A380, the primary 787 safety systems are grouped into the Rockwell Collins integrated surveillance system (ISS).

Acting as the combined ears and eyes of the aircraft, the ISS incorporates into a single unit the various systems that provide warnings about collisions with terrain and other aircraft, weather radar and constant reports of the aircraft's position. By integrating them into one box, Rockwell saved weight, volume, power consumption and cost.

Compared to a suite of equivalent federated systems, the ISS saves around 36% in weight, 26% in power consumption and an impressive saving of 60% in size. "Integrated surveillance is here to stay," said Rockwell Collins Senior Director of Airline Marketing Bryan Vester.

"With this platform, we're looking forward to the communications, navigation and surveillance/air-traffic management environment of the future for systems like ADS-B (automatic dependent surveillance-broadcast) and traffic computers," he said. "Working with those sorts of functions, the ISS will be part of the 'containment' and will help the 787 stay within the envelope it is supposed to be in, as well as protect it from anyone else who might try to enter its airspace."

The 787 will have two identical ISS cabinets. Each will contain the functionality of the traffic collision avoidance system (TCAS), Mode S transponders, terrain awareness warning system (TAWS) and weather radar. The TCAS warns of the approach of other aircraft and, if it predicts the potential for a collision, warns the crew and provides information on the best escape routes.

Mode S transponders continuously provide positioning reports to air traffic control and TAWS compares the aircraft's real-time position with a digital terrain database giving instant warning on the presence of any nearby high ground or obstacles such as towers and masts.

Rockwell Collins is developing the TCAS, Mode S and radar, which is based on the company's MultiScan hazard weather detection system (see page 137). Honeywell has been contracted to provide the TAWS.

The data from all the sensors is integrated and prioritized by a special computer in the surveillance system, dubbed the ISS 2100 processor.

From a safety and operational perspective, the presence of two identical cabinets meant that the 787 came ready-equipped with dual functionality. "It means that a 'hot spare' is part of the basic kit on the aircraft," Sinnett said. Although some airlines argued initially that the provision of the ISS as standard equipment "took their choice away", Sinnett said most have since recognized that "by making it basic and eliminating the variability [of options], we've reduced cost to the point where it provides the best economic choice."

Eye in the sky

The crew of the 787 will be able to scan well ahead more than 320nm for threatening turbulence and violent storms using the latest version of Rockwell Collins' WXR-2100 MultiScan nose-mounted weather radar.

Unlike many previous generations of weather radar, the 787 system will automatically hunt for any nasty conditions ahead, saving the crew from the tedious duty of manually altering the tilt angle of the radar – or the angle at which the receive/transmit antenna is pointed relative to the flight path. Instead, the radar is fully automatic and runs through a series of pre-programmed multiple tilt-angle scans and analyses the threat potential ahead of the aircraft using advanced radar signal processing. This is all without any pilot intervention and represents the way of the future, according to the maker.

The "smart" radar will constantly vary between short- and long-range weather detection scans without requiring pilot adjustment of the radar tilt. It will also alert flight crews during take-off and approach of potentially dangerous wind-shear – a sometimes troubling phenomenon involving sudden changes in wind speed and direction.

This "SmartScan" technology allows for rapid updates in turns, even though multiple beams of information are being collected. During turns, when flight crews would be momentarily blind to the weather towards which the aircraft is turning, the MultiScan solves this problem by using SmartScan to scan just in the direction of the turn, thus ensuring quick re-visit times. Weather information that is falling off the trailing edge of the display is "pasted-in" from digital memory to provide a complete weather picture. As a result, even though MultiScan uses multiple scans to build a complete weather picture, update rates in turns are as fast, or faster, than current generation radars.

Other features will include "overflight" protection, which will help crews to avoid inadvertent penetration of thunderstorm tops. According to Rockwell Collins, this is one of the main causes of unexpected turbulence encountered. Intelligent software in the processor will use signal data to measure storm-top height, as well as provide information about storm-cell development. MultiScan uses a combination of lower and upper beam information and computer memory to keep the thunderstorm top in view until it passes behind the aircraft.

Another feature which aids weather detection at all ranges but particularly near the "radar horizon" is ground clutter suppression. This allows the equipment to "look down" into ground clutter and "observe" the most reflective part of the storm cell with incredible radar strength of 20,000 watts!

It's a gas – inerting technology

The 787 is the first Boeing airliner to be equipped from the start with a fuel tank inerting system that will safeguard against the possibility, no matter how remote, of a spark igniting fumes in a partially empty fuel tank.

Safety experts decided to adopt the system as part of the baseline design after it was discovered that fumes in partially empty tanks could cause explosions in extremely rare circumstances. Such explosions are suspected of being the cause of the Trans World Airlines 747-100 crash in 1996 (TWA 800) and the destruction of a Thai Airways International 737-400 in Bangkok in 2001.

An inerting system replaces air in the partially empty tanks with nitrogen, preventing the ignition of oxygen-rich fuel vapors in the fuel tank ullage. The system works by pumping air through a molecular sieve designed to concentrate nitrogen. The collected nitrogen is then pumped into the tanks as the fuel is gradually used up over the course of a flight.

Hamilton Sundstrand, which is already a major provider of the 787 effort having multiple responsibilities for the electrical power generation, auxiliary power unit (APU), power distribution and environmental control systems, was awarded the work as part of its overall role. It subcontracted the inerting task to two divisions of UK-based Cobham: FR-HiTemp and Iowa-based Carleton Life Support Systems.

FR-HiTemp, which was also working on fuel transfer pumps for the 787, joined forces with Carleton, a well-known supplier of on-board inert gas generating systems (OBIGGS) to a host of military aircraft types, ranging from the Boeing AH-64 Apache and CH-47 Chinook helicopters to the C-17 Globemaster III transport.

"We had all sorts of technology choices to look at and different ways to inert but we have selected a brand-new design," Sinnett said. "Now we have a group that has come together to put a system on the aircraft that reduces the flammability of all the tanks all the time. That's a different approach to that of any other production model."

The 787 is the first Boeing airliner designed with a fuel tank inerting system that will safeguard against the possibility of a spark igniting fumes in a partially empty fuel tank. *Boeing*

The 787 cockpit can be powered from eight different sources.
Boeing

Back-up power by the barrel full

Not surprisingly for a "more-electric" aircraft, the 787 is provided with a powerful and robust set of emergency back-up systems.

"We designed the electrical system with a higher assurance level than ever before," Sinnett said. "We have six very large generators [mounted on the engines and auxiliary power unit], and we have a unique way of being able to power almost any load on the aircraft from one source."

The chief back-up emergency power device for the system is a Hamilton Sundstrand-developed ram air turbine (RAT), which "is similar to that used on the 777 but is different in that it is a hybrid with the ability to provide both electrical and hydraulic power," Sinnett explained.

The RAT is a small, windmill-like device that can be lowered from an enclosed bay usually found in the belly or wing-root area. As the system is normally deployed in an emergency, there is no guarantee of power being available to actuate the RAT into the slipstream, so it is designed to free-fall under gravity. The RAT is able to withstand deployment at any part of the flight envelope and will provide power to several systems, such as the engine start, the avionics and the flight controls.

The 787 is also the first commercial aircraft to use a lithium-ion (Li-ion) battery system, which provides more efficient energy storage than standard nickel-cadmium (NiCad) cells. Electrical systems on board the aircraft will require a range of standard voltages, and Li-ion technology will be implemented in the 787's electrical power conversion system supplied by France-based aerospace company Thales.

The system will automatically adjust variable-rate power from the aircraft's engines into standard voltage levels that can be used by the on-board systems. Japanese battery manufacturer, GS Yuasa, was selected by Thales to provide the Li-ion batteries for APU starting power and emergency power back-up.

Prototypes of the battery system were expected to be delivered to Thales in 2005 and production was set to begin in 2007. Li-ion batteries provide twice the storage capacity of NiCad cells of the same dimension and can be charged to 90% of capacity in 75 minutes and require no maintenance.

GKN Aerospace and UK-based Ultra Electronics will provide the 787's wing ice-protection system. *Boeing*

Defrosting the big freeze

Since the beginning of manned flight, one of the ever-present dangers has been the presence of atmospheric icing.

If an aircraft encounters super-cooled liquid in the form of cloud, rain or drizzle and the temperature of the surface of the airframe is below 0°C, icing can occur.

Ice can do drastic things to the flying characteristics of aircraft, particularly when it begins to stick to the leading edges of the wings. If even a relatively small layer of ice begins to accumulate, the resulting airflow disruption can reduce the maximum lift of the wing by as much as 50%!

As a consequence, the stalling speed also can increase and, because the aircraft has to fly at a greater angle-of-attack to maintain lift, the induced drag increases and the aircraft continues to lose airspeed. This makes flying at the same altitude difficult and has a disastrous impact on fuel consumption. Other potentially nasty effects include added weight, damage to external antennae and sensors and potential jamming or restricting of control surfaces.

To protect its "new baby" from these dangers, Boeing once again adopted an innovative solution. Instead of the traditional de-icing methods, which normally rely on heating the leading edges of the wing with hot air bled from the engines, Boeing chose an electro-thermal anti-ice system. Working with GKN Aerospace, UK-based Ultra Electronics was selected to provide the wing ice-protection system and was the lead contractor on the effort, responsible for overall integration, control software and electronic equipment.

GKN Aerospace was selected to provide the composite mat for the wing ice-protection system, which was based on non-bleed technology originally developed for helicopters and other applications, ranging from the Bristol Britannia to the Concorde. The system comprised a sprayed metal matrix element encapsulated by polymer composite materials fixed on, or in, the wing leading edges.

An electro-thermal system is required for the 787 because it does not use "bleed air" extracted from the engine to power systems. GKN originally developed electro-thermal anti-icing systems for helicopter blades, propeller spinners, flight-control surfaces and engine and equipment inlets. The system was also introduced on

the Eurocopter EH101 and Bell Boeing V-22 Osprey. The 787 was the first commercial application of this technology.

"It is a significant development," Sinnett said, who added that each section of the wing leading edge slat is protected by six individual heating mats, all independently controlled. "If you have a partial failure in the wing de-icing system, normally you have to deactivate it because of the potential asymmetry it could cause [more lift from one wing than the other]. With this approach, we're able to continue to operate because of the multiple-control of mats on each slat," he said.

GKN Aircraft Transparency Systems Vice President, Phil Harris said: "This means you put the heat where and when you want it, rather than the old hot gas system in which you just switch it on and let it flow." Colin Ross, Managing Director of Ultra Electronics Controls Division, added: "We expect this system to produce a similar level of heat but because it is electronically controlled, we can tailor it to operate either as an anti-ice system (in which ice is prevented from forming) or, if a generator or engine fails – we can go to a de-icing mode (in which ice is allowed to form before being broken up by the heat from the system)."

chapter17
Testing a Super Jet

In flying, I have learned that carelessness and over-confidence are usually far more dangerous than deliberately accepted risks.
— Wilbur Wright —

The greatest test ever

In line with safety and dependability, the 787 is also designed for remarkable longevity and, with its composite primary structure, could set the record somewhere in the far-off distant future for years in continuous service.

"We are creating an airplane that will appeal to literally billions of people," said Walt Gillette, Vice President 787 Airplane Development. "We think there is a market for around 3,500 aircraft in this sector and we have a reasonable chance of getting half that market. So, assuming we end up selling almost 2,000, and by the time the last one starts down into retirement, the 787 fleet will have carried 15 to 20 billion people! It is hard to make an airplane that the world will value and use for so long but this aircraft will be in service in the early years of the 22nd century. I truly believe that," he added.

The certification of the 787 is therefore expected to be one of the most grueling tests of an aircraft's structure and systems ever undertaken. The extensive use of composite materials, advanced more-electric systems and new architectures mean the testing would be a step beyond that undertaken by Boeing on any commercial venture before.

Boeing's planned testing for the 787 builds on a legacy going back to the early years of aviation when more rudimentary evaluations were made. To modern eyes, these often bordered on the bizarre – in the 1920s, structural wing testing consisted of production workers standing on the wing!

In 1932, while aircraft design had advanced considerably, structural testing had not, so Douglas was forced to use a steamroller driven across the wing to test the structural integrity of its DC-1 wing. Component level tests were just as basic, with the established test procedure for helmets pre-1920 consisting of the wearer running full tilt at the nearest brick wall!

Testing matured slowly to match the increasingly complex aircraft structures and systems but it still took some major shocks to push the state of the art. Fuselage pressure and fatigue testing, for example, was introduced after the de Havilland Comet crashes in the early 1950s revealed the potential problems of pressurization, high altitude and high cycles common with commercial jets.

In the exhaustive tests at Farnborough in the UK that followed the Comet 1 crashes, a Comet airframe was immersed in a giant tank and water was pumped in and out to simulate pressure changes with altitude. Eventually, a tiny crack developed near the corner of a window frame and, without sufficient strengthening, the airframe failed.

Today, the industry spends billions testing aircraft in every conceivable flight and structural condition, building to a large extent on the lessons learned from the tragic mistakes of the past.

In 1932, structural testing was basic, as this photo of a steamroller testing the strength of the DC-1 wing, shows.
Boeing Historical Archives

There will be many similarities between the testing done for the 777 (pictured) and the 787. *Boeing*

The science of testing

New aircraft enter service today only after every system and every part of their structure have been thoroughly probed, cooled, heated, stretched, pulled, squeezed and pummeled over and over again.

Testing begins long before the first real aircraft even comes together. Individual parts or material specimens and smaller elements are tested first, gradually working up to larger assemblies and major components. This practice, which had evolved in an ad hoc way over the years, was formalized into a rigorous, fully integrated process for the first time with the 777 program.

In recognition of the increased sophistication of the new jet, Boeing realized it would need to tackle testing in a more structured and holistic way. As a result, in the early 1990s, the company spent $370 million on an Integrated Aircraft Systems Laboratory (IASL).

The role of the IASL was to test the entire aircraft's systems, which were laid out in 46 labs. The plan was that each of the systems would be tested separately and then integrated into the "complete aircraft". This level of testing was needed to meet the rigorous demands of United Airlines, which wanted the 777 to be certified to 180-minutes Extended-Range Twin Operations (ETOPS) from the day it entered service.

The IASL lab tested nearly 60 major aircraft systems and more than 23,000 parts on the 777. Structures such as the undercarriage, which weighed 10,400lb (4,545kg), were tested 40,000 times. The tests "smoked out" problems that might not otherwise have been seen until either flight tests or in actual service. Boeing believed it was easily more cost-effective to spend money up front on the IASL than work with suppliers in far more expensive re-designs and re-working down the line.

Tests in the electrical power generation lab, for example, uncovered more than 40 problems that would otherwise only have been identified once the aircraft took to the air. When all the separate systems testing was done, the parts were linked to simulate real flight in a "super lab" called the System Integration Lab (SIL). The linked product was "test flown" twice a day, and at its peak, clocked up 400 "very short" flights a day during the latter half of 1992.

"There will be a lot of similarities between the testing done for the 777 and the 787," said Chief Project Engineer 787 Program Tom Cogan. "Although the quantity of testing will be very similar, the difference is that the tests will be more efficient, which will hopefully be reflected in a shorter flight-test program. We're going to have increased use of sensors and we will tap into the digital databus for extra test data. We are also working with partners to get instrumentation [for flight testing] installed earlier in the program. Flight-test wiring will be installed on parts of the first aircraft before final assembly," he added.

Testing to destruction

Every new aircraft must prove that its structure can withstand not only the day-to-day repetitive strains of flying and the cumulative effect this may have on the bare bones of the fuselage and wings but also that it can cope with meeting the once-in-a-lifetime flight loads that it might experience in service.

"Ground testing will be very similar to the 777, irrespective of any differences in materials or systems," said Cogan, who added that new technology will be in areas such as the use of laptops to monitor data, rather than desktop PCs.

As with other models, two substantially complete 787 airframes will be taken off the line and allocated to the static and fatigue tests. The static tests, which are generally timed to coincide with initial flight tests, are aimed at working out the sheer strength of the basic structure.

The 787 static test will closely follow the 777 airframe specimen, which was tortured on a giant rack-like rig using 96 hydraulic actuators applying loads from 0 to 100% in 20% intervals. Rates were typically increased by 5% per minute, while fuselage pressure was applied during tests to simulate flight load conditions.

The final, and most dramatic test, is bending the wings upwards beyond the ultimate load (or 1.5

times the load limit) to the point of destruction. On the 777, this point was reached when the wingtips were deflected more than 24ft above their normal position while enduring loads equal to around half a million pounds!

"It made a really loud noise and you could literally feel the pressure wave coming across the room," recalled Mike Sinnett, Life Cycle Product Team (LCPT) Leader and Chief Engineer Systems 787. "At normal cruise conditions, we expect it to have similar bending characteristics with just a few minor differences," Cogan said.

The second series of tests evaluate the fatigue life of the 787. The overall fatigue life of the aircraft is the time at which the repair of the structure is no longer economically feasible. It basically "sets the clock" for service use of the airframe. The 777 was severely punished in 120,000 simulated flights – or double the aircraft's expected life cycle. The 787, on the other hand, is being designed for a service life of 55,000 cycles, so will be fatigue-tested for 165,000 flights or three times the equivalent lifetime.

As with the 777, each "flight" is expected to last about four minutes during which the fuselage is pumped with air to a pressure representative of the 6,000ft cabin altitude of the composite fuselage. The flight will consist of taxiing, climbing, cabin pressurization and depressurization, descending and landing. To add realism, Boeing will also mix up the flights, from completely smooth and level to extremely turbulent.

Flight test

After coming through the structural and systems tests successfully, the next hurdle for the 787 is the flight-test program. Ironically, some of the most rigorous tests will occur on the ground.

No story about flight testing a commercial jet aircraft is complete without reference to the most famous Boeing test pilot of all, the legendary "Tex" Johnston. Not strictly speaking on a test flight at all, Tex was piloting Boeing's Dash-80 707-prototype for a demonstration fly-by for delegates attending the 1955 International Air Transport Association (IATA) annual general meeting in Seattle.

Boeing hosted delegates at the Gold Cup power boat races on Lake Washington and company president Bill Allen thought it would be a golden opportunity to impress the chiefs of the world's airlines. Instead of a sedate fly-past, to everyone's amazement, Tex put the Dash-80 into a 1g roll which, while not overstressing the airframe, gave Allen severe heart palpitations.

Not content with one roll, and in case any of the airline executives thought they were seeing things, Tex brought the Dash-80 around again and repeated the maneuver. The next day, legend has it that Tex quipped to Allen, when asked about the barrel roll, "I was just selling airplanes".

Although hoping to avoid any such dramatic maneuvers during the 787 test program, Boeing is none-the-less planning to throw the new jetliner around the sky in ways that it will never experience in service. As with the testing of the 777, the 787 will be a mammoth effort covering a similar amount of test hours but in a shorter time.

Once the Rolls-Royce Trent 1000-powered 787 effort starts in 2007, the test pace is expected to be far more rapid than any previous program. "We are going to double-crew the aircraft," Cogan said. "The goal is to increase the number of flying hours per day. We want those test airplanes flying as much as possible."

The General Electric GEnx-powered version would follow its sibling into the air within a few months. According to Cogan, "the two certification programs are pretty close and by the time the GEnx-program is underway we will have Rolls-Royce powered aircraft in the flight-test inventory."

Photo taken from the inverted Dash 80 (707 prototype) as it performed the famous barrel roll in 1955 with the city of Seattle below. *Boeing Historical Archives*

The spectacular Vmu test with the 777 sitting on its tail before lifting off. *Boeing*

Don't do this with your car

Once basic airworthiness and handling qualities have been established, the real business of opening the flight envelope begins.

This "exploration" maps out the maximum and minimum capabilities of the aircraft's performance in terms of speed and altitude with every combination of conditions and payloads imaginable.

Leading the flight-test program is Mike Carriker, Chief Test Pilot of the 787. Carriker spends more time in design meetings talking about how airplanes should fly and how pilots should interact with the airplane than actually flying. But he is convinced that those meetings are what will make the 787 a great success.

"Over the last 30 years, test pilots have gone from just taking the airplane as it was designed and testing it, to having an important role in design decisions from the very earliest days of the program," he said.

Mike Carriker *Boeing*

"The responsibility of a test pilot is symbolized in the first flight of the airplane,"Carriker said. "The whole team is focused on what we are doing and what we need to do next. But there is that moment when you call for take-off that you realize you have the hopes and ambitions of the entire company with you, that you have the backing of hundreds of thousands of people."

One of the most visually impressive tests, said Carriker, is the velocity minimum unstuck (Vmu) test, which determines the aircraft's minimum lift-off speed. The test pilot rotates the aircraft

under the normal take-off speed with a result that the aircraft "sits" on its tail before lifting off.

Another tortuous test is the rejected take-off test. The 787 is loaded to its maximum take-off weight and brought up to take-off speed. Without using reverse thrust, the pilot brings it to a stop using the electric brakes only. To add to the difficulty of the test, the 787's brakes will be degraded to the point of replacement. After stopping, the brakes become so hot they glow red but no action can be taken for five minutes, representing the time taken to get emergency vehicles to the aircraft.

Other tests will involve Boeing searching the world for the worst weather conditions. Typically, the cold-soak tests are performed in Sweden and Alaska, while New Mexico and Alice Springs in Australia provide searing temperatures – and more than a few flies. For crosswind landings, it will be off to wherever the correct conditions can be found – maybe Alaska, Idaho, Scotland or Iceland.

Royal Air Maroc announced its intention to order five 787s in August 2005. *Boeing*

Trusty power plants

The new engines for the world's most advanced airliner were both destined to fly for the first time on the world's first wide-body, the 747.

In the case of Rolls-Royce, which had not operated its own dedicated flying test bed for many years, the 747 was seen as a vitally necessary investment for testing the 787's Trent 1000. Boeing had resurrected the venerable 747 prototype, the RA001, from its slumbers to test the Trent 800 and PW4072 engines for the 777 in the early 1990s but that famous aircraft had since been permanently retired.

A 747 was therefore acquired and converted by Texas-based L-3 Communications – a specialist in complex 747 modifications having developed aircraft as diverse as SOFIA, the airborne 747SP-based flying astronomical observatory and the US Presidential aircraft VC-25A "Air Force One".

Rolls-Royce began assembling the first Trent 1000 in early November 2005 and was expected to begin test runs in February 2006 with first flight on the 747 within a month or so after that. Engine certification was set for mid-2007 and entry into service, with 787 launch customer All Nippon Airways, was scheduled for mid-2008.

Seven engines were due to take part in the ground-test effort and an eighth power plant was allocated for service reliability work as part of Boeing's target of achieving ETOPS clearance at entry into service.

General Electric (GE) expected to start assembly of the first GEnx engine in October 2005, with first engine to test in March 2006. Tests on GE's 747-100 flying test bed (FTB) were set for the third quarter of 2006, with first flight on the 787 expected about a year later.

The GE test bed was one of the oldest 747s still flying, being an ex-Pan American machine and the 16th off the Everett line.

Up to 10 test engines were assigned to the certification program. Seven were assigned to the 787 and the balance were for the bleed-enabled version for the Airbus A350-800/900.

Engine tests for both companies followed the same fundamental format, covering basic operability, exploration of stall and surge margins, performance throughout the flight envelope and critical work on fuel consumption monitoring.

Ground tests meanwhile explored the ability of the engine to cope with deluges of water, simulating flight through a once-in-a-hundred-years storm, battering hail and flocks of birds. The tests culminated with the dramatic fan blade-off test in which a blade is released at maximum power by setting off an explosive charge buried in its roots.

The tests ensured that, just like the aircraft flight tests, the engines would prove to be remarkably reliable workhorses for the newest airliner of the 21st century.

Specification and Orders

Specifications

	787-3	787-8	787-9
Length	182ft (56m)	182ft (56m)	202ft (62m)
Height	54ft	54ft	54ft
Wingspan	165-170ft	193ft	193ft
MTOW	360,500lb	476,000lb	508,500lbs
Passengers*	296/2 class	224/3 class	259/3 class
Engines - GEnx	GEnx-54B	GEnx-64B	GEnx-70B
Thrust	53,200lb	63,800lb	69,800lb
Engines - Trent 1000	-E1 & -H1	-A1 & -G1	-C1 & -D1
Thrust	53-58,000lbs	64-67,000lbs	70-70,000lbs plus
Maximum Range**	3,500nm	8400nm	8200nm
Speed	Mach 85	Mach 85	Mach 85
Launch date	26th April 2004	26th April 2004	2005
First Flight	2009	Mid 2007	2009
First Delivery	2010	Mid 2008	2010

Passengers*: Based on most luxurious interior configuration with seats and aisles wider than 747 or 777.
Passenger numbers would increase significantly if airlines adopt a 3-3-3 configuration in economy which gives 747 comfort levels.
Maximum Range**: Typical range with standard passenger configuration plus luggage.
The above 787 and engine figures are provisional and are subject to change.

Orders

	Country	Model	Number	Engine
All Nippon Airways	Japan	787-3	30	Rolls-Royce
All Nippon Airways	Japan	787-8	20	Rolls-Royce
Air New Zealand	New Zealand	787-8	2	Rolls-Royce
Blue Panorama Airlines	Italy	787-8	4	
First Choice Airways	UK	787-8	6	GEnx
Japan Airlines	Japan	787-3	13	Rolls-Royce
Japan Airlines	Japan	787-8	17	Rolls-Royce
Continental Airlines	USA	787-8	5	
Korean Air	South Korea	787-8	10	
Ethiopian Airlines	Ethiopia	787-8	10	
Icelandair	Iceland	787-8	2	
Northwest Airlines	USA	787-8	18	
Unidentified Customer		787-8	6	
Total			**143**	

Contracts to be concluded

	Country	Model	Number	Engine
Vietnam Airlines	Vietnam	787-8	4	
Primaris Airlines	USA	787-8	20	
Continental Airlines	USA	787-8	5	
Air China	China		15	
China Eastern	China		15	
Shanghai Airlines	China		9	
Xiamen Airlines	China		3	
China Southern	China		10	
Hainan Airlines	China		8	
Air India	India	787-8	20	
Royal Air Maroc	Morocco	787-8	5	
Total			**257**	

Bibliography

Adams, H.W. *The Inside Story: The Rise and Fall of Douglas Aircraft* Toledo Publishing, Batangas, Philippines, 2000

Airbus Industrie *Twins Through Time* Toulouse, France, 1989

Bauer, E.E. *Boeing: The First Century* TABA Publishing Inc., Washington, USA, 2002

Brooks, P. W. "Transport Aircraft Development: Parts 1, 2 and 3" *AIR Pictorial*, Profile Books Ltd., London, UK, May, June and July 1985 issues

Davies, R.E.G. *Airlines of the United States since 1914* Putnam and Co. Ltd., London, UK, 1972

Davies, R.E.G. *A History of the World's Airlines* Oxford University Press, London, 1967

European Low Fare Association *"Liberalization of European Air Transport 2004"* Brussels, Belgium

Francillon, R.J. *McDonnell Douglas Aircraft since 1920* Putman and Co. Ltd., London, UK, 1979

Gann, H. *Douglas DC-6 and DC-7* Specialty Press, MN, USA, 1999

Greenwood, J.T. (ed.) *Milestones of Aviation* Hugh Lauter Levin Assoc. Inc., New York, USA, 1989

Gunston, B. "A Tale of Two Rivers" *AIR International*, Key Publishing Ltd., Stamford, UK, April 2001 issue

Hardy, M.J. *The Lockheed Constellation* David and Charles (Holdings) Ltd., Devon, UK, 1973

Holden, Henry M. *The Douglas DC-3* Airlife Publishing Ltd., England, 1991

Ingells, D.J. *L-1011 TriStar and the Lockheed Story* Aero Publishers Inc., Cal., USA, 1973

Ingells, D.J. *747: Story of the Boeing Super Jet* Aero Publishers Inc., California, USA, 1970

Jarrett, P. *Modern Air Transport: Worldwide Air Transport from 1945 to the Present* Putnam Aeronautical Books, London, UK, 2000

Morrison, W.H. *Donald W. Douglas: A Heart with Wings* Iowa University Press, USA, 1991

Newhouse, J. *The Sporty Game: The high-risk competitive business of making and selling commercial airliners* Alfred A. Knopf, New York, USA, 1982

Norris, G. and Wagner, M. *Boeing 777: The Technological Marvel* MBI Publishing Co., WI, USA, 2001

Orlebar, C. *The Concorde Story: Fifth Edition* Osprey Publishing, Oxford, UK, 2002

Pearcy, A. *Douglas Propliners DC-1 - DC-7* Airlife Publishing Ltd., Shrewsbury, UK, 1995

Pugh, P. *The Magic of a Name: The Rolls-Royce Story. Part Three: A Family of Engines* Icon Books Ltd., Cambridge, UK, 2002

Ramsden, J.M. *The Safe Airline* MacDonald and Jane's Publishers Ltd., London, UK, 1976

St. John Turner, P. *Pictorial History of Pan American World Airways* Ian Allan Ltd., London, UK, 1973

Stringfellow, C.K. and Bowers, P.M. *Lockheed Constellation: Design, Development, and Service History of all Civil and Military Constellations, Super Constellations, and Starliners* Motorbooks International, Wisconsin, USA, 1992

Szurovy, G. *Classic American Airlines* MBI Publishing Co., Wisconsin, USA, 2000

Taneja, Professor Nawal *FASTEN YOUR SEAT BELT: The Customer is Flying the Plane* Ashgate, London United Kingdom 2005

Thomas, G. and Forbes Smith, C. *Flightpaths: Exposing the myths about airlines and airfares* Aerospace Technical Publications International, Western Australia, 2004

Upton, J. *Lockheed L-1011 Tristar* Specialty Press, MN, USA, 2001

Veronico, N.A. *Boeing 377 Stratocruiser* Specialty Press, MN, USA, 2001

Waddington, T. *Douglas DC-8: Volume 2* World Transport Press, Florida, USA, 1996

Waddington, T. *McDonnell Douglas DC-9* World Transport Press, Florida, USA, 1998

Whitford, R. "Fundamentals of Airliner Design: Parts 1, 2, 3, 9, 10, 12" *AIR International* Key Publishing Ltd., Stamford, UK. February 2001, April 2001, June 2001, June 2002, August 2002, January 2003, issues

Yenne, B. *Classic American Airliners* MBI Publishing Co., MN, USA, 2000

Yenne, B. *The Story of the Boeing Company* AGS BookWorks, CA, USA, 2003

Yule, P. *The Forgotten Giant of Australian Aviation: Australian National Airways* Hyland House Publishing Pty Ltd., Flemington, Australia, 2001

Index